GLOBE EDUCATION SHAKESPEARE

MUCH ADO ABOUT NOTHING

William Shakespeare

DYNAMIC LEARNING

S-E-T

Dear Leistungskurs-Students!
Don't blame Shakespeare!

Patrick Spottiswoode

Shakespeare did not write his plays to be read in a classroom!

He wrote his comedies and tragedies for actors to play on a stage.
He could never have imagined that students in England – let alone in Germany – would one day be reading his plays in school, or that his plays would be performed in theatres across the world.

Reading a play without seeing it in performance is difficult in any language. Reading a Shakespeare play when English is not your mother tongue is a tremendous challenge.

Shakespeare does not give lectures. He asks questions but does not offer answers. There can never be a definitive production of a play. Every production is but one response to the text and the result of interpretative choices made by directors, actors, musicians and designers. A performance also requires an audience! At the Globe audiences are particularly important as characters can speak directly to them as they crowd around the stage.

This edition aims to support your reading of the play by providing examples of three very different interpretations of *Much Ado About Nothing* that have been staged at the Globe Theatre. I hope the video clips, the interviews with actors and directors and the practical exercises from the rehearsal room will also help stimulate your own responses to the play.

I also hope you will be inspired to see a live Shakespeare performance in Germany or even at the Globe Theatre in London.

I am very grateful to S-E-T Studienreisen Bremen for publishing this edition in Germany for Leistungskurs students.

The play is the thing.....

Patrick Spottiswoode
Director, Globe Education, London

Dear Students, Dear Teachers!
We are very fortunate that since 1997 we have had the wonderful opportunity of being able to see Shakespeare's plays in a reconstructed Globe Theatre.

The original Globe, the very theatre for which Shakespeare wrote many of his plays, burned to the ground in 1613.

Globe Education, the new Globe Theatre's education department, every year inspires thousands of students from Germany with lively and practical introductions to Shakespeare's language, his plays and his theatre.

Do join us on this journey and you will discover that Shakespeare is as relevant for us today as he was 400 years ago!

Heinz Abeling
S-E-T Studienreisen, Bremen

A guided tour of the Globe Theatre.

"Unser Shakespeare"
A lecture-performance for Oberstufe-Students

In this very lively and humorous presentation actors and practitioners from Globe Education introduce students to Shakespeare, his plays, his life and his time.

Vivid story-telling, wit, humour and audience participation are the key ingredients of this "lecture", which has been specifically designed for German Oberstufenschüler.

It gives a fascinating account of the Globe and of London some 400 years ago and it also includes a guided tour of the reconstructed Globe Theatre.

"Unser Shakespeare"

"Unser Globe"
A drama-workshop for Mittelstufe-Students

Speaking, listening, laughing, acting and communicating: these are the ways students meet Shakespeare.

Throughout this drama-workshop students are on their feet, working as playfully with language as Shakespeare intended.

It is difficult to introduce Shakespeare to students in rectangular classrooms at rectangular desks. The words were written to be played and students want to get up and play!

"Unser Globe"

Shakespeare and the Globe

Shakespeare was born in 1564, in Stratford, a small town in the Midlands. We know he was still in Stratford as an eighteen-year old, when he got married. By 1592, he had moved to London, become an actor, and become a playwright. Shakespeare died in Stratford in 1616. He probably retired three or four years earlier, having bought land, and the biggest house in the town.

Shakespeare was successful. He became a shareholder in his acting company, and a shareholder in the Globe – the new theatre they built in 1599. His company was the best in the land, and the new king, James I, made them his company in 1603. They were known as the King's Men. Men, because women were not allowed to act on the stage. Boys or men played all the women's parts. Shakespeare wrote at least 40 plays, of which only 38 survive. Only eighteen of his plays were printed in his lifetime, including *Much Ado About Nothing*. After his death, his colleagues published a collection of 36 of his plays, known as the *First Folio*.

London Theatres

There were professional companies of actors working in London from the middle of the sixteenth century. They usually performed in inns, and the city council often tried to ban them. The solution was to have their own purpose-built theatre, just outside the area the council controlled. The first, simply called *The Theatre*, opened in 1576.

Shakespeare's Globe today

Sam Wanamaker, an American actor and director, founded the Shakespeare's Globe Trust in 1970. Sam could not understand why there wasn't a proper memorial to the world's greatest playwright in the city where he had lived and worked. He started fundraising to build a new Globe Theatre. Sadly, Sam died before the theatre opened in 1997.

The new Globe is the third. The first burnt down in 1613 during a performance of Shakespeare's *Henry VIII*. The King's Men rebuilt it on the same site, and it re-opened in 1614. This second one was closed in 1642, and pulled down in 1647 to build houses.

The new Globe is 200 yards from the original site, and is based on all the evidence that survives. It has been built using the same materials as the original, and using the same building techniques.

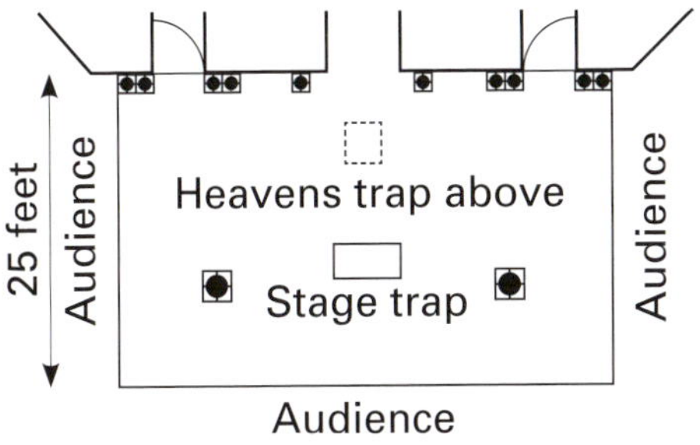

The stage trap opened into the area under the stage. The heavens trap was not on the stage, but above it. Actors playing gods might be lowered down to the stage through it.

The first Globe Theatre

The Globe Theatre was open-air. If it rained, some of the audience got wet. There was no special lighting; so the plays were performed in the afternoon, in daylight. This meant that, unlike most modern theatres, the actors could see the audience, as well as the audience see the actors (and each other). It may have held as many as 3,000 people, with, perhaps, 1,000 standing in the yard. Those standing paid one old penny (there were 240 in £1). The rest sat in the three galleries, so they were under cover if it rained. They paid more, at least two pence, and as much as six pence for the best seats. The audience was a mixture of social classes, with the poorer people standing.

The stage was large, and extended into the middle of the yard, so there were people on three sides. We think it had three entrances in the back wall – a door on either side, and a larger one in the middle. There was a roof so the actors, and their expensive costumes, would always be in the dry. The underside of this roof, called *the heavens*, was painted with the signs of the zodiac. There was also an upper stage, which was sometimes used in plays, sometimes used by the musicians, and also had the most expensive seats in the theatre. All the rest of the audience could see people who sat in the upper stage area. If you sat there, people could see who you were, that you could afford to sit there, and your expensive clothes.

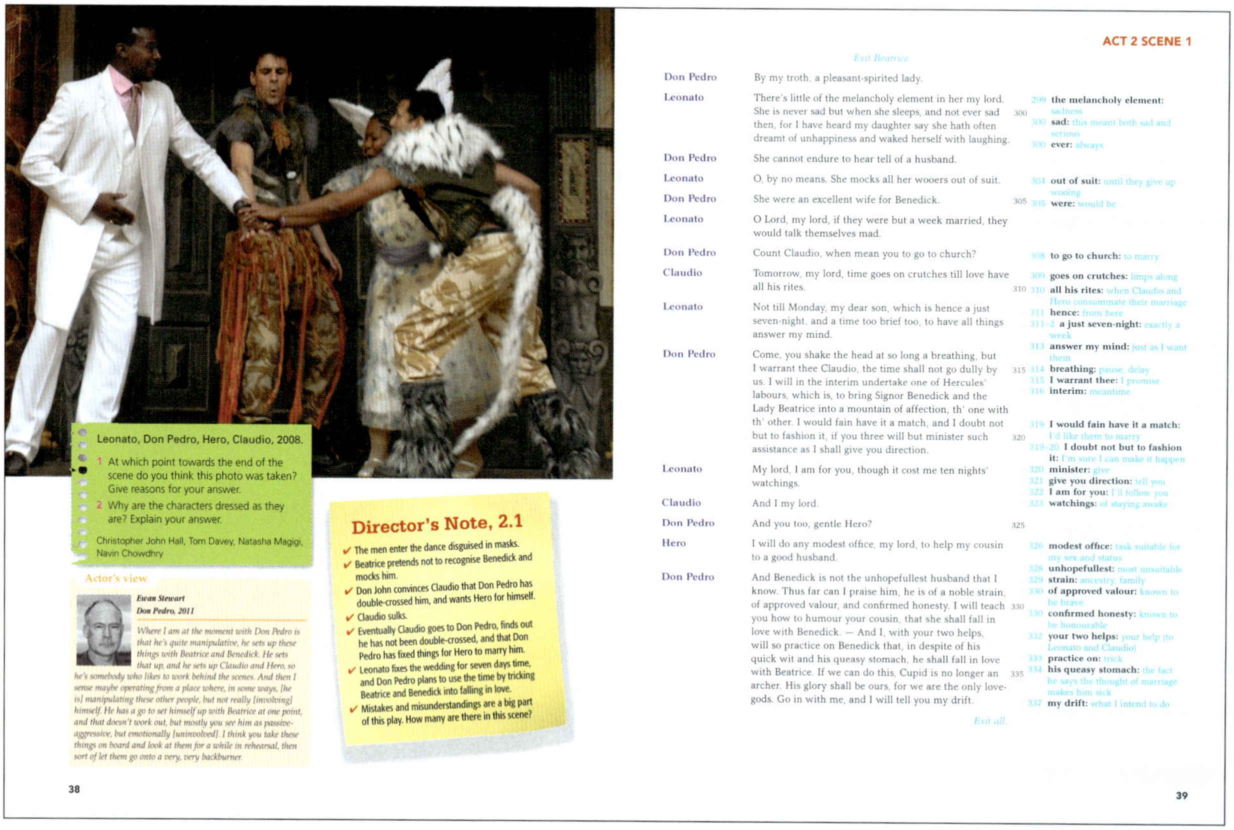

The **play text** is the place to start. What characters say is in black, and stage directions are in blue. Line numbers, on the right, help you refer to an exact place.

Leonato	*[To Don Pedro.]* Please it your Grace lead on?
Don Pedro	Your hand Leonato, we will go together.
	Exit all except Benedick and Claudio.
Claudio	Benedick, didst thou note the daughter of Signor Leonato?
Benedick	I noted her not, but I looked on her.

Some stage directions, like the first one above, have square brackets. This means they are not in the original text, but have been added to help you when you read. They tell you what you would see on the stage.

116 **A bird of my tongue … a beast of yours:** I may chatter like a bird, you are as dumb as a beast

The **glossary** is right next to the text. To help you find the word or phrase you want, each entry has the line number in blue, then the word or phrase in black, and finally the explanation in blue again. To keep it clear, sometimes, as in this case, some words from the original have been missed out, and replaced with three dots.

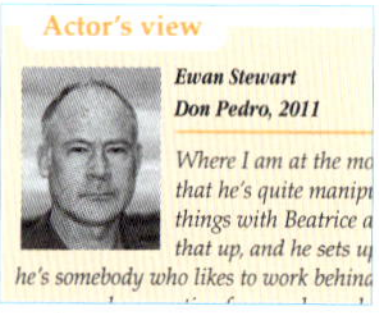

Actor's view boxes are exactly what they say. Actors who have played the part at the Globe tell you what they thought about their character and some of the choices they made.

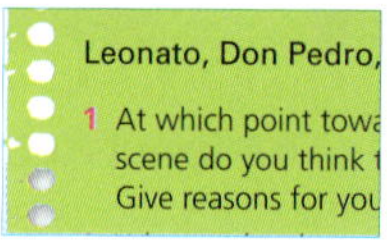

Green boxes go with the photos. They tell you what you are looking at, and give you a question to think about. Unless the question says otherwise, the answer will be in the play text on the opposite page. The names of the actors are in smaller print.

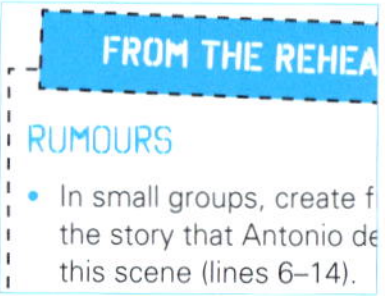

From the rehearsal room gives you the exercises actors use during rehearsals to help them understand the play. They come with questions that help you reflect on what you can learn from the exercise.

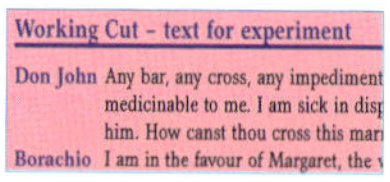

Working Cuts sometimes go with the *From the rehearsal room* activities. They cut lines from the scene so you can do the activity in the time you have available.

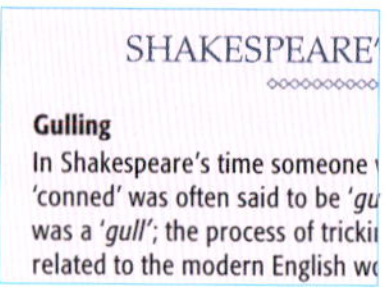

Shakespeare's World boxes give you important context for the play. For example, 'gulling' is an expression we are not familiar with nowadays. Understanding context like this will improve your understanding of the play.

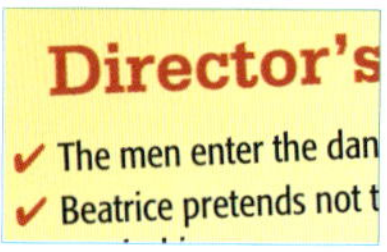

Finally, **Director's Note** boxes come at the end of every scene. They give you a quick summary of the most important things in the scene, and a focus to think about.

The Characters in the play

This book uses photographs from three productions of *Much Ado About Nothing* at Shakespeare's Globe. The actors and creative teams of each production are an important part of the book.

	2004 *Director: Tamara Harvey*	**2008** *Director: Joanne Howarth*	**2011** *Director: Jeremy Herrin*
Leonato's Household			
Leonato, Governor of Messina	Penelope Beaumont	Christopher John Hall	Joseph Marcell
Antonio, Leonato's brother	Penelope Dimond		John Stahl
Hero, Leonato's daughter	Mariah Gale	Natasha Magigi	Ony Uhiara
Beatrice, Leonato's niece	Yolanda Vazquez	Kirsty Besterman	Eve Best
Margaret, gentlewoman to Hero	Joy Richardson	Rachel Spence	Lisa McGrillis
Ursula, gentlewoman to Hero	Lucy Campbell		Helen Weir
The soldiers			
Don Pedro, Prince of Aragon	Belinda Davison	Tom Davey	Ewan Stewart
Claudio	Ann Ogbomo	Navin Chowdhry	Philip Cumbus
Benedick	Josie Lawrence	Bill Buckhurst	Charles Edwards
Balthasar, a singer	Joyce Henderson		David Nellist
Don John, bastard brother of Don Pedro	Rachel Sanders	Tom Stuart	Matthew Pidgeon
Borachio, follower of Don John	Gabrielle Reidy	Mark Rice-Oxley	Joe Caffrey
Conrade, follower of Don John	Hannah Barrie		Marcus Griffiths
Messenger			David Nellist
People of Messina			
Friar Francis	Jules Melvin	Tony Taylor	Joe Caffrey
Dogberry, master constable	Sarah Woodward	Tony Taylor	Paul Hunter
Verges, his assistant	Jules Melvin	Rachel Spence	Adrian Hood
George Seacole, one of the Watch	Joyce Henderson		David Nellist
Hugh Oatcake, one of the Watch	Joy Richardson		John Stahl
Sexton	Lucy Campbell	Tom Stuart	Matthew Pidgeon
Servants, members of the Watch, musicians			
Designer	Luca Costigliolo	Liz Cooke	Mike Britton
Composer	Claire van Kampen	Alex Silverman	Stephen Warbeck
Choreographer	Siân Williams	Siân Williams	Siân Williams
Musical Director	Belinda Sykes	Emily White	David Powell

SHAKESPEARE'S WORLD

The war

The men arriving at Leonato's house in this opening scene have come from the battlefield. A war has finished. Don Pedro has been fighting, probably against his brother, Don John. This is not certain, but is suggested by Leonato, who says that Don John is now 'reconciled to the prince your brother'.

We are not told how long the war has been going on and we never find out what the causes of it were. We do know that in the final battle 'few of any sort, and none of name' from Don Pedro's side have died. Whilst this sounds positive, it applies only to the high-ranking soldiers. The words 'sort' and 'name' both refer to upper-class status. How many ordinary soldiers died does not matter to the messenger, or to Leonato.

Many members of an Elizabethan audience would have been to war. England in the 1580s and 1590s was engaged in many conflicts with other countries in Europe. Those men who had been in battle would understand the close relationships between the men in the play. The experiences of war – fighting and surviving together – have formed a bond, of trust and of companionship, which the events of the play will test severely.

In the 2011 production, the family came on before the messenger. Here Beatrice and Hero (behind) relax.

What impression does the photo give the audience of what life was like for Hero and Beatrice?

Ony Uhiara, Eve Best

SHAKESPEARE'S WORLD

Beatrice in her uncle's house

Beatrice lives with her uncle Leonato and his daughter, her cousin Hero. In Elizabethan society, a single woman did not have the same privileges as a man. Families often sent their daughters to live with relatives to widen their social circle and to improve their marriage prospects. If a woman's father and brothers had died, she normally lived with a close male relative such as an uncle.

MUCH ADO ABOUT NOTHING ACT 1 SCENE 1

Enter Leonato, Governor of Messina; Hero, his daughter; and Beatrice, his niece, with a messenger.

Leonato I learn in this letter that Don Pedro of Aragon comes this night to Messina.

Messenger He is very near by this. He was not three leagues off when I left him.

Leonato How many gentlemen have you lost in this action?

Messenger But few of any sort, and none of name.

Leonato A victory is twice itself when the achiever brings home full numbers. I find here that Don Pedro hath bestowed much honour on a young Florentine called Claudio.

Messenger Much deserved on his part, and equally remembered by Don Pedro. He hath borne himself beyond the promise of his age, doing in the figure of a lamb the feats of a lion. He hath indeed better bettered expectation than you must expect of me to tell you how.

Leonato He hath an uncle here in Messina, will be very much glad of it.

Messenger I have already delivered him letters, and there appears much joy in him, even so much that joy could not show itself modest enough without a badge of bitterness.

Leonato Did he break out into tears?

Messenger In great measure.

Leonato A kind overflow of kindness, there are no faces truer than those that are so washed. How much better is it to weep at joy than to joy at weeping?

Beatrice I pray you, is Signior Mountanto returned from the wars or no?

Messenger I know none of that name, lady. There was none such in the army of any sort.

Leonato What is he that you ask for, niece?

Hero My cousin means Signor Benedick of Padua.

Messenger O, he's returned, and as pleasant as ever he was.

Beatrice He set up his bills here in Messina and challenged Cupid at the flight. And my uncle's fool, reading the challenge, subscribed for Cupid and challenged him at the birdbolt. I pray you, how many hath he killed and eaten in these wars? But how many hath he killed? For, indeed, I promised to eat all of his killing.

Leonato Faith niece, you tax Signor Benedick too much, but he'll be meet with you, I doubt it not.

Messenger He hath done good service, lady, in these wars.

nothing: used here as a pun. It could mean 1) nothing; 2) a slang reference to the vagina at the time – 'no-thing'; 3) at the time it could be pronounced the same as 'noting' – to see or to observe

3 **by this:** by now
3 **three leagues:** about 9 miles (14 km)
5 **action:** battle
6 **But few of any sort:** not many noblemen or gentlemen
7 **the achiever:** the person who leads the winning army
8–9 **bestowed much honour on:** given many rewards to
10 **equally remembered:** suitably rewarded
12–3 **doing in the figure of a lamb the feats of a lion:** showing the courage of an experienced soldier, despite his youth and inexperience
13–4 **better bettered expectation ... to tell you how:** done so much better than anyone could have expected – I can't begin to tell you how much more
18 **even so much:** so very much
19 **a badge of bitterness:** tears

22 **kind:** affectionate

31 **pleasant:** amusing
32 **set up his bills:** put up posters
32–3 **challenged Cupid at the flight:** challenged the god of love to an archery contest: suggests 1) he won't fall in love; 2) he's made more ladies fall in love than Cupid
34 **subscribed for Cupid:** took up the challenge for Cupid
35 **birdbolt:** a blunt arrow
38 **tax:** criticise
39 **be meet:** get even

'Enter Don Pedro, Claudio, Benedick, Balthasar, and Don John (the Bastard).'

***A* 2008:** the men entered through the yard singing a military song. Bill Buckhurst, Navin Chowdhry

***B* 2011:** the men also entered through the yard before climbing onto the stage to meet the women. *l to r:* Eve Best, Ony Uhiara, Joseph Marcell, Ewan Stewart, Philip Cumbus, Charles Edwards

1 How does each production show the men are coming from a war? Explain your answer.

2 The 2008 production (A) was in modern dress, while the 2011 production (B) was in the dress of the time. What are the advantages and disadvantages of using modern dress?

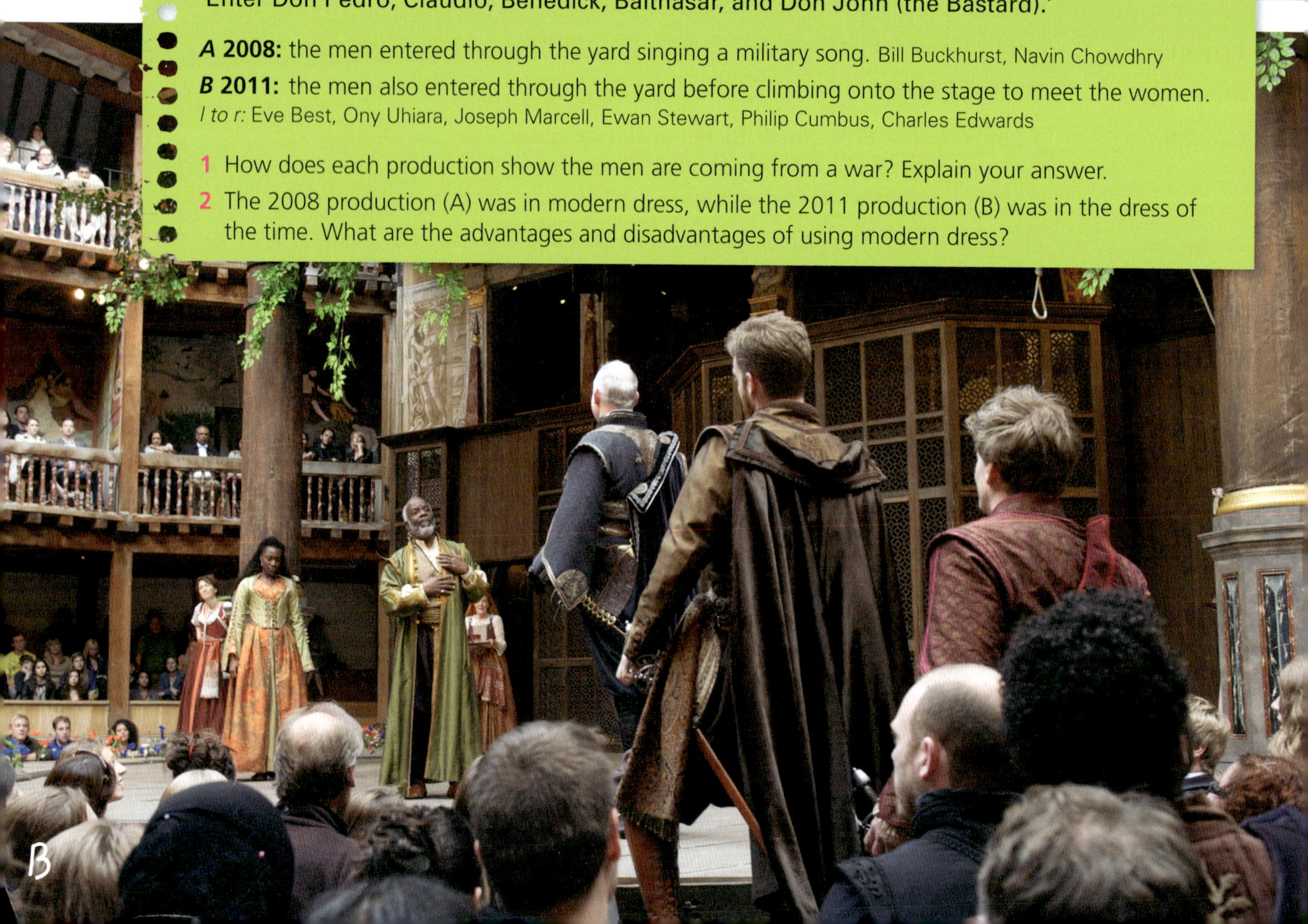

Beatrice You had musty victual, and he hath holp to eat it. He's a very valiant trencherman, he hath an excellent stomach.

Messenger And a good soldier too, lady.

Beatrice And a good soldier to a lady. But what is he to a lord?

Messenger A lord to a lord, a man to a man, stuffed with all honourable virtues.

Beatrice It is so indeed? He is no less than a stuffed man. But for the stuffing — well, we are all mortal.

Leonato You must not, sir, mistake my niece. There is a kind of merry war betwixt Signor Benedick and her. They never meet but there's a skirmish of wit between them.

Beatrice Alas, he gets nothing by that. In our last conflict four of his five wits went halting off, and now is the whole man governed with one. So that if he have wit enough to keep himself warm, let him bear it for a difference between himself and his horse, for it is all the wealth that he hath left to be known a reasonable creature. Who is his companion now? He hath every month a new sworn brother.

Messenger Is't possible?

Beatrice Very easily possible. He wears his faith but as the fashion of his hat, it ever changes with the next block.

Messenger I see, lady, the gentleman is not in your books.

Beatrice No, and if he were, I would burn my study. But I pray you, who is his companion? Is there no young squarer now that will make a voyage with him to the devil?

Messenger He is most in the company of the right noble Claudio.

Beatrice O Lord, he will hang upon him like a disease! He is sooner caught than the pestilence, and the taker runs presently mad. God help the noble Claudio! If he have caught the Benedick, it will cost him a thousand pound ere he be cured.

Messenger I will hold friends with you, lady.

Beatrice Do, good friend.

Leonato You will never run mad, niece.

Beatrice No, not till a hot January.

Messenger Don Pedro is approached.

Enter Don Pedro, Claudio, Benedick, Balthasar, and Don John (the Bastard).

Don Pedro Good Signor Leonato, you are come to meet your trouble. The fashion of the world is to avoid cost, and you encounter it.

41 **musty victual:** stale food
41 **holp:** helped
42 **valiant:** brave
42 **trencherman:** eater
42 **stomach:** appetite
44 **to:** compared to/when faced with
47 **a stuffed man:** a tailor's dummy or scarecrow – not a real man
51 **skirmish of wit:** battle of words
53 **halting:** limping
55–6 **let him bear it for a difference:** that's a difference he can show exists
56–7 **all the wealth that he hath left to be known:** all he possesses to show he is
59 **sworn brother:** close comrade in the army he has sworn to treat like a brother
61 **faith:** loyalty
62 **block:** a piece of wood that hats were shaped on – hats of one shape could be wetted and reshaped on a block
63 **books:** good books; favour
64 **study:** library
65 **squarer:** troublemaker; keen for a fight
68 **hang upon:** stick to
69 **the pestilence:** the plague
69 **the taker:** the person who has caught it
70 **presently:** instantly
71 **the Benedick:** pretending it is a disease
72 **ere he be:** before he is
75 **You will never run mad:** you will never fall for Benedick
77 **is approached:** has arrived
SD **(the Bastard):** illegitimate son – see page 23
79 **trouble:** refers to the trouble of having Don Pedro and the others come to stay
80 **encounter it:** put yourself out to meet it

An all-female production

In Shakespeare's time plays were performed by all-male casts – men and boys took the women's roles. The modern Globe normally casts men and women, but it has experimented with all-male casts, and also with all-female casts. In the production of *Much Ado About Nothing* in 2004 women took all the roles.

Benedick and Beatrice, 2004.

This photograph was taken between lines 93 and 120.

1. Which character was speaking, Benedick or Beatrice? Give reasons for your answer.
2. Pick a line or phrase that you think is most likely to be the one being spoken at the exact moment the photograph was taken, and explain the reasons for your choice.

Josie Lawrence, Yolanda Vazquez

FROM THE REHEARSAL ROOM...

STRICTLY POINT SCORING

Read the first long exchange between Beatrice and Benedick (lines 93–120).

- Work in small groups, with each group split into two – *Team Beatrice* and *Team Benedick*. Each team chooses one person to read their character's lines, and the rest of the team are listeners.
- The two readers read from line 93 to line 120. The listeners keep score of the insults their character says – one point for each insult.

1. Who has the most points at the end?
2. Agree one remark as the winning insult. What makes it the winner?

FROM THE REHEARSAL ROOM...

LOVE ON THE LINE

You have to decide how Beatrice and Benedick feel about each other **at this point in the play** (line 120). Imagine there is a line drawn across your classroom like the one below. The closer Beatrice and Benedick are to the middle, the more they are in love with the other.

- In pairs, discuss the text and decide where each of them is on the line.
- Stand in that place on the line. Compare your choices with other people's. Support your points with quotations from the text.

1. Record your answer, and the one that the majority of the class agree on. Quote from the text to support your view.

Leonato Never came trouble to my house in the likeness of your Grace, for trouble being gone, comfort should remain. But when you depart from me, sorrow abides and happiness takes his leave.

Don Pedro You embrace your charge too willingly. I think this is your daughter?

Leonato Her mother hath many times told me so.

Benedick Were you in doubt, sir, that you asked her?

Leonato Signior Benedick, no, for then were you a child.

Don Pedro You have it full, Benedick. We may guess by this what you are, being a man. Truly, the lady fathers herself. Be happy lady, for you are like an honourable father.

[Don Pedro and Leonato talk privately.]

Benedick If Signor Leonato be her father, she would not have his head on her shoulders for all Messina, as like him as she is.

Beatrice I wonder that you will still be talking, Signor Benedick, nobody marks you.

Benedick What, my dear Lady Disdain! Are you yet living?

Beatrice Is it possible Disdain should die while she hath such meet food to feed it as Signor Benedick? Courtesy itself must convert to disdain, if you come in her presence.

Benedick Then is courtesy a turncoat. But it is certain I am loved of all ladies, only you excepted, and I would I could find in my heart that I had not a hard heart, for truly I love none.

Beatrice A dear happiness to women, they would else have been troubled with a pernicious suitor. I thank God and my cold blood, I am of your humour for that. I had rather hear my dog bark at a crow than a man swear he loves me.

Benedick God keep your ladyship still in that mind! So some gentleman or other shall 'scape a predestinate scratched face.

Beatrice Scratching could not make it worse an 'twere such a face as yours were.

Benedict Well, you are a rare parrot-teacher.

Beatrice A bird of my tongue is better than a beast of yours.

Benedick I would my horse had the speed of your tongue, and so good a continuer. But keep your way, i' God's name, I have done.

Beatrice You always end with a jade's trick. I know you of old.

Don Pedro *[Ending his talk with Leonato.]* That is the sum of all, Leonato. Signior Claudio and Signior Benedick, my dear friend Leonato hath invited you all. I tell him we shall stay here, at the least a month, and he heartily prays

---

82 **for:** because
83 **abides:** remains
85 **embrace your charge:** accept this heavy responsibility
89 **for then were you a child:** you were only a child then (implying Benedick is a ladies' man who women fall for)
90 **have it full:** asked for that
91 **fathers herself:** is clearly her father's daughter from her looks
93–4 **his head:** an old man's head
97 **marks you:** pays you any attention
100 **meet food to feed it:** a suitable target for distain
100 **Courtesy itself:** even the personification of politeness
101 **come in her presence:** come near her
102 **turncoat:** someone who changes sides
106 **dear happiness:** lucky thing
106 **else:** otherwise
107 **troubled with a pernicious suitor:** pursued by a man it is dangerous to have a relationship with
108 **I am of your humour for that:** I, like you, don't fall in love
110 **still in that mind!:** always of that opinion
111 **'scape:** escape
111 **predestinate:** unavoidable
113 **an 'twere:** if it was
115 **are a rare parrot-teacher:** do chatter on and on
116 **A bird of my tongue ... a beast of yours:** I may chatter like a bird, you are as dumb as a beast
118 **so good a continuer:** could keep going as long as you keep talking
118 **keep your way:** you just carry on
120 **a jade's trick:** the behaviour of a worthless horse, stopping suddenly
120 **I know you of old:** I'm used to your ways

Leonato greets Don John (lines 128–9), 2011.

In this production, right from the start, Don John seems to be an outsider. Which of the actors above do you think is playing Don John?

Joseph Marcell, Marcus Griffiths, Matthew Pidgeon, Ewan Stewart

SHAKESPEARE'S WORLD

Courting

People were advised to court someone of their own age and social status for a successful marriage. Frequently, parents suggested a match, often for financial and social reasons. Young people certainly flirted, but courtship was a more formal process. Leonato shows the distinction between mere flirtation and courtship when he declares that he expects his daughter to be formally courted by her suitors. Early on in courtship, if not before it began, the man was expected to tell the bride's father he was thinking of marriage. They then negotiated the bride's dowry (money and gifts given to the groom when they married) and her jointure – money and land that would be given to her if she became a widow. The groom's father often took part in these negotiations.

While it seems unromantic today, courtship in Shakespeare's day involved more people than just the future bride and groom. Every couple treated courtship differently, but they usually began by finding out more about each other. It was unacceptable for a woman to be alone with a suitor, so courting couples usually had friends, servants or family members present. This was to prevent sexual activity before marriage. Many suitors wrote letters to their intended spouse. Courting couples usually exchanged gifts. Such gifts were a signal to others that the couple was discussing marriage, or negotiating its terms. A man traditionally gave a woman he was courting gloves, ribbons or coins. Suitable tokens were sometimes included in the bride's attire on the wedding day. At times, men used messengers or servants to deliver letters, tokens or messages to a lady. This can be seen in Shakespeare's plays as well. In *Othello*, Cassio is used as a go-between when Othello is wooing Desdemona. The length and formality of courtship varied between couples, but it typically lasted for at least a few months. In this play, Hero and Claudio's courtship takes place quickly. They have had very little time to get to know each other.

some occasion may detain us longer. I dare swear he is no hypocrite, but prays from his heart.

Leonato If you swear, my lord, you shall not be forsworn. *[To Don John.]* Let me bid you welcome, my lord. Being reconciled to the prince your brother, I owe you all duty.

Don John I thank you. I am not of many words, but I thank you.

Leonato *[To Don Pedro.]* Please it your Grace lead on?

Don Pedro Your hand Leonato, we will go together.

Exit all except Benedick and Claudio.

Claudio Benedick, didst thou note the daughter of Signor Leonato?

Benedick I noted her not, but I looked on her.

Claudio Is she not a modest young lady?

Benedick Do you question me, as an honest man should do, for my simple true judgment? Or would you have me speak after my custom, as being a professed tyrant to their sex?

Claudio No, I pray thee speak in sober judgment.

Benedick Why, i' faith, methinks she's too low for a high praise, too brown for a fair praise, and too little for a great praise. Only this commendation I can afford her, that were she other than she is, she were unhandsome, and being no other, but as she is, I do not like her.

Claudio Thou think'st I am in sport. I pray thee tell me truly how thou lik'st her.

Benedick Would you buy her, that you enquire after her?

Claudio Can the world buy such a jewel?

Benedick Yea, and a case to put it into. But speak you this with a sad brow? Or do you play the flouting Jack, to tell us Cupid is a good hare-finder and Vulcan a rare carpenter? Come, in what key shall a man take you to go in the song?

Claudio In mine eye, she is the sweetest lady that ever I looked on.

Benedick I can see yet without spectacles, and I see no such matter. There's her cousin, an she were not possessed with a fury, exceeds her as much in beauty as the first of May doth the last of December. But I hope you have no intent to turn husband, have you?

Claudio I would scarce trust myself, though I had sworn the contrary, if Hero would be my wife.

Benedick Is't come to this? In faith, hath not the world one man but he will wear his cap with suspicion? Shall I never see a bachelor of threescore again? Go to, i' faith, an thou wilt needs thrust thy neck into a yoke, wear the print of it, and sigh away Sundays. Look, Don Pedro is returned to seek you.

---

127 **be forsworn:** be proved a liar by anything I do

128 **Being:** since you are

133 **didst thou note:** did you see

135 **noted her not:** didn't pay her any special attention

139 **after my custom:** as I usually do

139 **a professed tyrant to:** one who is openly harsh against

141 **too low:** too short

142 **too brown:** her skin's too dark

143 **commendation:** praise

143 **afford:** give

144 **were she other than … unhandsome:** if she looked different, she wouldn't be good-looking (i.e. she is good-looking)

146 **in sport:** messing around

148 **Would you:** do you want to

151 **with a sad brow:** seriously

151 **flouting Jack:** fool

152–3 **Cupid is a good … carpenter:** outrageous lies (Cupid was blind; Vulcan was a blacksmith)

153–4 **Come, in what key … in the song:** explain your mood, so I can join in

157–8 **she were not possessed with a fury:** if she wasn't so bad tempered and angry

164 **but he will wear his cap with suspicion:** who isn't willing to marry and risk being a cuckold (see page 19)

165–6 **an thou wilt needs thrust … yoke:** if you really must tie yourself down

167 **sigh away Sundays:** become a family man and bored

left Benedick; *right* Claudio, 2011. Both photos were taken while the characters we talking about women and love in the text opposite.

1 What does their body language and expression suggest about their attitudes to women and love?

2 Which line or lines do you think each was saying when the photo was taken? Explain your answer.

Charles Edwards, Philip Cumbus

Actor's view

Philip Cumbus
Claudio, 2011

The relationship with Claudio and Hero is nice to explore. As two people who are about to get married they barely know each other at all. She doesn't know me and I don't know her, so that sets up a nice tension. He speaks about how he knew her a little bit and had seen her, but what I have been finding very interesting is Claudio's change in himself. I don't think, on many levels, that Claudio believes he is fully worthy of such a beautiful and virtuous lady as Hero, until he comes back from the war, and he's been newly hailed as this great victor in the war, and has been treated as a success. And that fuels in Claudio a new confidence that possibly he hasn't had [before]. So suddenly, riding on that wave of celebration, he maybe feels now that he can possibly obtain someone as lovely as Hero. Whereas before I think he was always too quiet, too shy and didn't have enough self-worth to pursue her.

Actor's view

Bill Buckhurst
Benedick, 2008

What we're discovering in rehearsals is the sort of laddish banter. I mean, I've heard conversations like this now-a-days like, 'What? You're not getting married! You can't get married! What are you doing? You're letting the lads down.' It's that kind of thing. This is a soldier who hangs out with lads the whole time, he's very comfortable with men, he's a bit of a joker, a bit of a laugh. He's up for fun and it's just not cool to be with a woman. Benedick's got a real thing about being a man and the minute you're with a woman it all changes. And the other thing, I think, which he talks about the whole time, the worst thing for a man at this time when Shakespeare is writing would be for the wife to go off and have an affair and [for him] to be cuckolded. Benedick makes many references to the idea of this in the play and I think for him he's so terrified that that would happen to him and it's become a real issue for him.

Enter Don Pedro.

Don Pedro What secret hath held you here, that you followed not to Leonato's?

Benedick I would your Grace would constrain me to tell.

Don Pedro I charge thee on thy allegiance.

Benedick You hear, Count Claudio. I can be secret as a dumb man, I would have you think so. But, on my allegiance, mark you this, on my allegiance, he is in love. With who? Now that is your Grace's part. Mark how short his answer is. With Hero, Leonato's short daughter.

Claudio If this were so, so were it uttered.

Benedick Like the old tale, my lord: "It is not so, nor 'twas not so, but indeed, God forbid it should be so!"

Claudio If my passion change not shortly, God forbid it should be otherwise.

Don Pedro Amen, if you love her, for the lady is very well worthy.

Claudio You speak this to fetch me in, my lord.

Don Pedro By my troth I speak my thought.

Claudio And in faith, my lord, I spoke mine.

Benedick And, by my two faiths and troths, my lord, I spoke mine.

Claudio That I love her, I feel.

Don Pedro That she is worthy, I know.

Benedick That I neither feel how she should be loved, nor know how she should be worthy, is the opinion that fire cannot melt out of me. I will die in it at the stake.

Don Pedro Thou wast ever an obstinate heretic in the despite of beauty.

Claudio And never could maintain his part, but in the force of his will.

Benedick That a woman conceived me, I thank her. That she brought me up, I likewise give her most humble thanks. But that I will have a recheat winded in my forehead, or hang my bugle in an invisible baldrick, all women shall pardon me. Because I will not do them the wrong to mistrust any, I will do myself the right to trust none. And the fine is (for the which I may go the finer) I will live a bachelor.

Don Pedro I shall see thee, ere I die, look pale with love.

Benedick With anger, with sickness, or with hunger, my lord, not with love. Prove that ever I lose more blood with love than I will get again with drinking, pick out mine eyes with a ballad-maker's pen, and hang me up at the door of a brothel house for the sign of blind Cupid.

171 **constrain:** force
172 **charge:** order
172 **on thy allegiance:** on the oath you swore to me as your lord
174 **I would have you:** I want you to
178 **If this were so, so were it uttered:** just like him to put it like that
184 **fetch me in:** trick me into saying too much
185 **By my troth:** I give you my word
192 **I will die in it at the stake:** I'll be publicly burned for my belief that women aren't worth loving
193–4 **heretic in the despite of beauty:** unbeliever, not accepting the power of beauty
195–6 **maintain his part, but in the force of his will:** follow this belief without a lot of willpower (sexual innuendo here)
199–200 **have a recheat winded … hang my bugle in an invisible baldrick:** be made a cuckold by a wife – a recheat was a hunting call sounded on a horn (a pun on cuckold's horn); a bugle was a word for a horn (with a double meaning of penis); a baldrick was a belt which held a sword
201 **pardon me:** excuse me
203 **fine:** conclusion
203 **go the finer:** be able to spend more on my appearance (with no wife to support)
207–8 **lose more blood with love … drinking:** get paler with love than I grow red with drinking
210 **for:** in place of

Don Pedro and Claudio, 2011.

This was taken during the first line of a Don Pedro speech, which follows Claudio speaking. Pick which Don Pedro line you think it is most likely to be, and give reasons for your choice.

Ewan Stewart, Philip Cumbus

SHAKESPEARE'S WORLD

Inheritance, women and property

One of the things negotiated by a suitor and the father of the possible bride was the dowry. The dowry was given by the bride's father to seal the marriage vows. It could be money, household objects or even inheritance rights. The inheritance of land passed from father to son. Women could not inherit property; instead it went either to their husband, or to the nearest male relative. Shakespeare's audience knew that by marrying Hero, Claudio would inherit both Leonato's property and his money when he died, because Hero was Leonato's only child so the inheritance would go to her husband.

Don Pedro Well, if ever thou dost fall from this faith, thou wilt prove a notable argument.

Benedick If I do, hang me in a bottle like a cat and shoot at me. And he that hits me, let him be clapped on the shoulder and called Adam.

Don Pedro Well, as time shall try:
"In time the savage bull doth bear the yoke."

Benedick The savage bull may, but if ever the sensible Benedick bear it, pluck off the bull's horns and set them in my forehead, and let me be vilely painted, and in such great letters as they write "Here is good horse to hire", let them signify under my sign. "Here you may see Benedick the married man."

Claudio If this should ever happen, thou wouldst be horn-mad.

Don Pedro Nay, if Cupid have not spent all his quiver in Venice, thou wilt quake for this shortly.

Benedick I look for an earthquake too then.

Don Pedro Well, you will temporize with the hours. In the meantime, good Signor Benedick, repair to Leonato's, commend me to him, and tell him I will not fail him at supper, for indeed he hath made great preparation.

Benedick I have almost matter enough in me for such an embassage, and so I commit you —

Claudio To the tuition of God.
From my house — if I had it —

Don Pedro The sixth of July.
Your loving friend, Benedick.

Benedick Nay, mock not, mock not. The body of your discourse is sometime guarded with fragments, and the guards are but slightly basted on neither. Ere you flout old ends any further, examine your conscience. And so I leave you. *Exit Benedick.*

Claudio My liege, your highness now may do me good.

Don Pedro My love is thine to teach. Teach it but how,
And thou shalt see how apt it is to learn
Any hard lesson that may do thee good.

Claudio Hath Leonato any son, my lord?

Don Pedro No child but Hero, she's his only heir.
Dost thou affect her, Claudio?

Claudio O my lord,
When you went onward on this ended action,
I looked upon her with a soldier's eye,
That liked, but had a rougher task in hand
Than to drive liking to the name of love.
But now I am returned, and that war-thoughts
Have left their places vacant, in their rooms

212 **notable argument:** talking point
213 **in a bottle like a cat:** cats were sometimes hung in a basket and used for archery practice
219–20 **and set them in my forehead:** a cuckold was supposed to have horns in his forehead
220 **let me be vilely painted:** have a bad portrait painted of me
224 **horn-mad:** raving mad (referring to the cuckold's horns)
225 **spent all his quiver:** used all his arrows
225 **Venice:** said at the time to be full of prostitutes, mistresses and adulterous wives
226 **quake:** shake; tremble with passion
228 **temporize with the hours:** change in time
230 **commend me to him:** give him my regards
230 **I will not fail him:** I will definitely be
233 **embassage:** mission
233 **I commit you …:** the start of a polite goodbye in letter writing – the next four lines carry on the joke
238–41 **The body of your discourse … examine your conscience:** the fabric of your speech has all sorts of frills and ornaments loosely sewn on. Think before you use any more worn out phrases
243 **My liege:** my lord
243 **do me good:** help me
244 **My love is thine to teach:** I'm willing to do this
245 **apt:** quick
249 **affect:** love
250 **went onward:** set out
250 **this ended action:** the war we've won
254 **that:** as
255 **in their rooms:** instead of them

Claudio and Don Pedro, 2011.

1 Which of the characters is leading the action on stage?
2 How well does this fit with what the two men are saying? Explain your answer.

Philip Cumbus, Ewan Stewart

Come thronging soft and delicate desires,
All prompting me how fair young Hero is,
Saying I liked her ere I went to wars.

Don Pedro
Thou wilt be like a lover presently,
And tire the hearer with a book of words.
If thou dost love fair Hero, cherish it,
And I will break with her and with her father,
And thou shalt have her. Was't not to this end
That thou began'st to twist so fine a story?

Claudio
How sweetly you do minister to love,
That know love's grief by his complexion!
But lest my liking might too sudden seem,
I would have salved it with a longer treatise.

Don Pedro
What need the bridge much broader than the flood?
The fairest grant is the necessity.
Look what will serve is fit. 'Tis once, thou lovest,
And I will fit thee with the remedy.
I know we shall have revelling tonight,
I will assume thy part in some disguise,
And tell fair Hero I am Claudio,
And in her bosom I'll unclasp my heart,
And take her hearing prisoner with the force
And strong encounter of my amorous tale.
Then after to her father will I break,
And the conclusion is, she shall be thine.
In practice let us put it presently.

Exit both.

257 **prompting me:** telling me
258 **ere:** before
260 **with a book of words:** by talking non-stop of your love
262 **break:** negotiate a marriage
263 **to this end:** to get me to do this
265 **minister to:** help
266 **complexion:** appearance
267 **lest:** in case
268 **I would have salved it with a longer treatise:** I wanted to explain it fully
269 **What need:** You don't need
269 **the flood:** the river
270 **fairest grant:** best gift
270 **the necessity:** what's wanted
271 **Look what will serve is fit:** whatever works is best
271 **'Tis once:** in short
272 **fit thee:** provide you
274 **assume thy part:** pretend to be you
276 **in her bosom:** privately
276 **unclasp my heart:** tell her I love her
281 **presently:** as soon as we can

Director's Note, 1.1

- ✔ Don Pedro returns, victorious, from the war. With him are Benedick and Claudio (who has become a hero in the war), and Don John, Don Pedro's Bastard brother, who has been his enemy.
- ✔ Leonato, the governor of Messina, invites Don Pedro and his friends to stay in his house.
- ✔ Benedick and Beatrice (Leonato's niece) go back to their old habit of scoring points off each other.
- ✔ Claudio falls in love with Hero, Leonato's daughter. He tells Benedick, who mocks him, and tells Don Pedro.
- ✔ Don Pedro takes him seriously and offers to help, by pretending to be Claudio at the masked ball, and asking Hero and Leonato if they will agree to a marriage.
- ✔ Is this a good plan?

SHAKESPEARE'S WORLD

A cuckold

A cuckold is a husband whose wife has been unfaithful to him. It is also a verb that describes this action. The wife and her lover 'cuckold' a man. Cuckolds appear frequently in the plays of Shakespeare and his contemporaries. They are usually the subject of jokes and teasing.

On the other hand, a woman betrayed by her husband was not called a cuckold. The term only applied to men. This tells us some important things about Shakespeare's world. A man being unfaithful was seen as less important. The man was the head of the household, and being cuckolded took away some of his power, making him look a fool.

Cuckolds were compared, mockingly, to a creature or bird (the word comes from the sound a cuckoo makes). By far the most common comparison was to suggest that a cuckold grew horns. Benedick and Claudio use this image of a cuckold's horns in this scene. It was so common that they do not even have to use the word 'cuckold' for the audience to understand their jokes.

STUDY NOTES, 1.1

TIP

Voice

A character may speak in many different ways according to who they are speaking to, and how they feel. A character's language may show signs of attitude or of feeling, so that an audience can tell if the character is worried, angry, curious, challenging or trying to persuade.

Voice is the kind of speech behaviour which is so typical of a character that an audience can recognise who is speaking from a small extract. This may be because of accent, dialect or a personal language habit.

For example, Beatrice frequently returns a comment with a deliberate change in meaning (lines 43–4):

'And a good soldier, too, lady.'

'And a good soldier to a lady. But what is he to a lord?'

1 Character and plot development

The opening scene of a play has to convey essential features of setting, characters and plot. Here, Shakespeare is not concerned with the place of setting (Messina) but he does make sure that the setting includes recent events because the events have an influence on the plot. He introduces some characters directly on stage and introduces others by talking about them.

1. How does Shakespeare establish that the events of the play take place immediately after a period of warfare? Find the words and phrases that show you this.
2. What does the Messenger's report and the request to Don Pedro (lines 248–268) tell the audience about Claudio's military skill and his emotional nature? Find words to support this.
3. In what ways does Beatrice's conversation with the Messenger convey her attitude to Benedick? Look at the words she uses.
4. Hero has only one line in the whole scene (line 30). How does this create a sense of difference between her and Beatrice?

2 Characterisation and voice: dramatic language

One of Shakespeare's skills as a dramatist is in writing speech which conveys mood, attitude and personality to the audience. For example, the following can all convey attitude and feeling:
Manner of address ('Sir …','Friends …','You fools …')
Habits of speech ('I …er ….You … um …')
Vocabulary ('Cor! Get an eyeful of her!'/'Indeed, she is not without charm').

5. By calling Benedick 'Signior Mountanto' (line 25) Beatrice is giving him a name which she has invented to suit him. How does her choice of this name show that she is mocking him?
6. Benedick addresses Beatrice as 'Lady Disdain' (line 98). Is this more or less insulting than her reference to him as 'Signior Mountanto'? What might these insults suggest about their real feelings?
7. What does Beatrice's final comment that 'You always end with a jade's trick' (line 120) suggest about their relationship so far? Why has Shakespeare used animal imagery here?

3 Themes and ideas

Themes are issues that the writer uses to create drama – for example, jealousy, revenge, honour or conflict in relationships. Ideas are the ways we understand and explain these recurring aspects of real life and fiction.

8. Conflict – the opening scene creates a battle of wits between Benedick and Beatrice. How far is this a matter of their personalities and how much a matter of a wider battle between men and women?
9. Love – Beatrice expresses her attitude to love and to men in lines 108–9. What attitude does she intend to convey here?
10. Marriage – Benedick makes several references to love and marriage (lines 164–7, 206–10, 218–223). What do these suggest about his attitude to both? Support your answer with key words and phrases.

STUDY NOTES, 1.1

4 Performance

Performance is what translates a printed text that can be read in private into an audible, visible and active experience which can be watched in public.

11 What gesture would you suggest to the actor playing Beatrice to accompany her first line (line 25)? Explain your choice.

12 How would you advise the Messenger to play his lines with Beatrice: a) as a man who patronises Beatrice by explaining why she should admire Benedick; or b) as a man who is slow to understand what Beatrice says and means? Explain your choice.

13 Would you advise Benedick in lines 93–120 to seem to be struggling to defend himself or enjoying the exchange of insults?

14 How might Claudio be performed – as a shy, emotional young man in love, a clumsy youth more concerned with himself than with Hero or a sincere man of passionate feelings? Explain your choice.

5 Contexts and responses

Some contexts are simply where an action takes place in the play – the setting. Other contexts are the medium in which the play is performed – on screen, on stage or in the classroom. Responses will vary from one person to the next, and are likely to reflect the taste, opinion and preferences of individuals in the audience.

15 In what ways does the final part of the scene, with Claudio and Don Pedro, suggest that women may not have had as much freedom as men in Messina (lines 243–81)? Find words from the text to support your answer.

16 Do you see Beatrice as a woman who has either:

a) too much to say for herself

b) more intelligence than the men around her?

Find evidence from the text to support your answer.

17 From what you have learned so far about the characters, how well suited do you think Benedick would be as a partner for:

a) Hero

b) Beatrice?

Explain your answer carefully and provide evidence from the text to support your answer.

6 Reflecting on the scene

18 What is there in this scene to suggest that Shakespeare makes Beatrice and Benedick very similar, despite their differences? Look at what they say and how they say it.

19 How has Shakespeare established his main characters in this opening scene, and given the audience hints about how the plot may develop? Look carefully at what the characters say.

20 How has your appreciation of this scene been enhanced by stage, screen or classroom performance?

USING THE VIDEO

Exploring interpretation and performance

If you have looked at the video extracts in the online version, try this question.

Joanne Howarth, the Director of the 2008 production, says there are two ways of interpreting the banter between Beatrice and Benedick:

a) as witty exchanges aimed at each other, *or*

b) as witty exchanges for the amusement of other characters on stage.

Looking at stage position, body posture and gesture, which interpretation do you think is shown in the clip: a, b, or both?

TIP

A good response

Show you are aware that characters are not real people by mentioning their creator: e.g. 'Shakespeare makes Beatrice seem sarcastic by giving her lines which mock Benedick's abilities and boastings as a soldier.'

Support your comment with a quotation: e.g. 'Shakespeare makes Beatrice seem sarcastic when she says "How many hath he killed and eaten in these wars?"'

Show that you understand why Shakespeare uses dramatic devices: e.g. 'Shakespeare makes Beatrice use exaggeration here to make it seem that she is repeating Benedick's exaggeration of the things he does as a soldier.'

ACT 1 SCENE 2

Enter Leonato and his brother, Antonio, an old man.

Leonato How now, brother, where is my cousin, your son? Hath he provided this music?

Antonio He is very busy about it. But brother, I can tell you strange news that you yet dreamt not of.

Leonato Are they good?

Antonio As the event stamps them, but they have a good cover, they show well outward. The Prince and Count Claudio, walking in a thick-pleached alley in my orchard, were thus much overheard by a man of mine. The Prince discovered to Claudio that he loved my niece your daughter, and meant to acknowledge it this night in a dance, and if he found her accordant, he meant to take the present time by the top, and instantly break with you of it.

Leonato Hath the fellow any wit that told you this?

Antonio A good sharp fellow. I will send for him, and question him yourself.

Leonato No, no. We will hold it as a dream till it appear itself. But I will acquaint my daughter withal, that she may be the better prepared for an answer, if peradventure this be true. Go you and tell her of it.

[Enter attendants, and Antonio's son, Balthasar, the musician.]

Cousins, you know what you have to do. — *[To the musician.]* O, I cry you mercy, friend. Go you with me, and I will use your skill. — Good cousin, have a care this busy time.

They all exit.

6 **As the event stamps them:** depending on how they turn out
6–7 **they have a good cover:** it looks as if they will be
8 **thick-pleached alley:** a tree-lined path where the trees meet overhead
10 **discovered to:** told
12 **accordant:** willing
13 **take the present time by the top:** seize the moment
15 **wit:** intelligence
18 **appear itself:** actually happens
19 **acquaint my daughter withal:** tell my daughter about it
20 **peradventure:** perhaps

Director's Note, 1.2

- ✓ Leonato's brother, Antonio, tells him a servant has overheard Don Pedro say he is in love with Hero, and that he plans to tell her at the dance, and, if she is willing, ask for Leonato's permission to marry her.
- ✓ The servant has got the story wrong, but does Leonato believe it?

FROM THE REHEARSAL ROOM...

RUMOURS

- In small groups, create freeze frames to illustrate the story that Antonio describes to Leonato in this scene (lines 6–14).
- Read the actual conversation in Act 1 Scene 1, lines 274–81. Compare it with Antonio's version.

1 How accurate was Antonio?

2 What does Leonato decide to do as a result of Antonio's information?

FROM THE REHEARSAL ROOM...

PORTRAIT OF DON JOHN

Look at Act 1 Scene 3, lines 8–14 and 22–31.

- In pairs, take it in turns to read each extract.
- Read it again, and make a list of adjectives that you think describe Don John's outlook on life and his personality.

1 Make a table with your adjectives in one column and the phrase (or word) from the text that made you choose it in the other column.

2 Pick one word to sum up Don John, and give reasons for your choice.

ACT 1 SCENE 3

Enter Don John the Bastard, and Conrade, his companion.

Conrade What the good-year, my lord! Why are you thus out of measure sad?

Don John There is no measure in the occasion that breeds, therefore the sadness is without limit.

Conrade You should hear reason.

Don John And when I have heard it, what blessing brings it?

Conrade If not a present remedy, at least a patient sufferance.

Don John I wonder that thou (being as thou say'st thou art, born under Saturn) goest about to apply a moral medicine to a mortifying mischief. I cannot hide what I am. I must be sad when I have cause, and smile at no man's jests, eat when I have stomach, and wait for no man's leisure, sleep when I am drowsy, and tend on no man's business, laugh when I am merry, and claw no man in his humour.

Conrade Yea, but you must not make the full show of this till you may do it without controlment. You have of late stood out against your brother, and he hath ta'en you newly into his grace, where it is impossible you should take true root but by the fair weather that you make yourself. It is needful that you frame the season for your own harvest.

Don John I had rather be a canker in a hedge than a rose in his grace, and it better fits my blood to be disdained of all than to fashion a carriage to rob love from any. In this (though I cannot be said to be a flattering honest man) it must not be denied but I am a plain-dealing villain. I am trusted with a muzzle and enfranchised with a clog, therefore I have decreed not to sing in my cage. If I had my mouth, I would bite. If I had my liberty, I would do my liking. In the meantime, let me be that I am, and seek not to alter me.

Conrade Can you make no use of your discontent?

Don John I make all use of it, for I use it only. Who comes here?

Enter Borachio.

What news, Borachio?

Borachio I came yonder from a great supper. The Prince your brother is royally entertained by Leonato, and I can give you intelligence of an intended marriage.

Don John Will it serve for any model to build mischief on? What is he for a fool that betroths himself to unquietness?

Borachio Marry, it is your brother's right hand.

Don John Who, the most exquisite Claudio?

Borachio Even he.

1 **What the good-year:** a mild oath – what the devil
1–2 **thus out of measure sad:** so very, very unhappy
3 **the … breeds:** the reason
7 **present remedy:** instant cure
7 **a patient sufferance:** the ability to put up with it patiently
8–9 **born under Saturn:** his horoscope suggests he was born with a gloomy nature
10 **mortifying mischief:** shameful circumstances
13 **tend on:** attend to
14 **claw no man in his humour:** flatter noone by following his whims
16 **without controlment:** freely
17 **stood out:** rebelled
17–8 **ta'en you newly into his grace:** just forgiven you
19–20 **take true … yourself:** earn his trust unless you work at it
20 **It is needful that you:** you must
22 **canker:** wild rose, the word also meant a sore or cancer
23 **my blood:** my illegitimate status
24 **fashion … to rob love:** pretend to be something I'm not to gain favour
27 **trusted with a muzzle:** only trusted if muzzled, like a fierce dog
27–8 **enfranchised … clog:** given limited freedom; tied to a block of wood
29 **If I had:** If I was free to use
33 **I use it only:** it is all I can think of
37 **intelligence:** news
38 **serve for any model:** can we use it
39 **unquietness:** a miserable life
40 **Marry:** 'By the Virgin Mary', used at the start of a sentence for emphasis as 'Well' is now

SHAKESPEARE'S WORLD

Bastards

Don John is Don Pedro's half brother. Their father married Don Pedro's mother, not Don John's. A child of married parents was 'legitimate' and had legal rights (such as inheriting his father's property). Don John is 'illegitimate' or, more simply, a 'bastard'. He would not inherit his father's property. Bastards were common figures in plays at this time. They were often shown as bitter, evil characters. They often plot against their legitimate brothers. Both Don John and Edmund in *King Lear* do this.

Don John A proper squire! And who, and who? Which way looks he?

Borachio Marry, on Hero, the daughter and heir of Leonato.

Don John A very forward March-chick! How came you to this?

Borachio Being entertained for a perfumer, as I was smoking a musty room comes me the Prince and Claudio, hand in hand in sad conference. I whipped me behind the arras, and there heard it agreed upon that the Prince should woo Hero for himself, and having obtained her, give her to Count Claudio.

Don John Come, come, let us thither. This may prove food to my displeasure. That young start-up hath all the glory of my overthrow. If I can cross him any way, I bless myself every way. You are both sure, and will assist me?

Conrade To the death, my lord.

Don John Let us to the great supper. Their cheer is the greater that I am subdued. Would the cook were of my mind. Shall we go prove what's to be done?

Borachio We'll wait upon your lordship.

They all exit.

43 **A proper squire:** A very suitable lover (said with contempt)
43 **Which way looks he?:** who does he want to marry?
45 **A very forward March-chick:** aiming so high, so young
46 **entertained:** employed
46 **for a perfumer:** a man who fumigated the rooms so they smelled sweet
46 **smoking:** perfuming
48 **sad conference:** serious conversation
48 **arras:** wall-hanging
53 **start-up:** upstart; pushy new-comer
54 **overthrow:** recent defeat
54 **cross:** hinder, make trouble for
55 **sure:** loyal
58 **Would the cook were of my mind:** if only the cook hated them too and was willing to poison them
59 **go prove:** go and find out

Director's Note, 1.3

- ✔ Don John is bitter about his defeat.
- ✔ Borachio tells him of the Don Pedro's plan to help Claudio marry Hero.
- ✔ Don John hates Claudio who had a big part in his defeat. He hopes to spoil the plan in any way he can.

ACT 2 SCENE 1

Enter Leonato; his brother, Antonio; Hero, his daughter; Beatrice, his niece; and Ursula and Margaret.

Leonato Was not Count John here at supper?

Antonio I saw him not.

Beatrice How tartly that gentleman looks. I never can see him but I am heart-burned an hour after.

Hero He is of a very melancholy disposition.

Beatrice He were an excellent man that were made just in the midway between him and Benedick. The one is too like an image and says nothing, and the other too like my lady's eldest son, evermore tattling.

Leonato Then half Signor Benedick's tongue in Count John's mouth, and half Count John's melancholy in Signor Benedick's face –

Beatrice With a good leg and a good foot, uncle, and money enough in his purse, such a man would win any woman in the world, if he could get her good will.

Leonato By my troth, niece, thou wilt never get thee a husband if thou be so shrewd of thy tongue.

Antonio In faith, she's too curst.

Beatrice Too curst is more than curst. I shall lessen God's sending that way, for it is said, "God sends a curst cow short horns", but to a cow too curst he sends none.

3 **tartly:** sour-faced
4 **am heart-burned:** have indigestion
8 **an image:** a statue
8–9 **my lady's eldest son:** a spoilt child
17 **shrewd:** sharp
18 **curst:** critical and given to arguing
19–21 **I shall lessen … he sends none:** I shall lessen the number of cuckolds in the world by not marrying

FROM THE REHEARSAL ROOM...

MORE RUMOURS

Read Borachio's lines 46–51 in Act 1 Scene 3.

- In small groups, create freeze frames that tell his story of Don Pedro and Claudio's conversation.
- Compare it with the actual conversation in Act 1 Scene 1 lines 274–81.

1 How has Borachio changed the story?

2 How could this version of the story affect the people involved?

FROM THE REHEARSAL ROOM...

BEATRICE AND MEN

- Read Beatrice's speeches that describe her attitude towards men and marriage (between lines 19 and 68 in Act 2 Scene 1).

1 What are her top five reasons not to marry? Quote from the text to support each reason.

Leonato So, by being too curst, God will send you no horns.

Beatrice Just, if he send me no husband, for the which blessing I am at him upon my knees every morning and evening. Lord, I could not endure a husband with a beard on his face. I had rather lie in the woollen!

Leonato You may light on a husband that hath no beard.

Beatrice What should I do with him? Dress him in my apparel and make him my waiting gentlewoman? He that hath a beard is more than a youth, and he that hath no beard is less than a man. And he that is more than a youth, is not for me. And he that is less than a man, I am not for him. Therefore I will even take sixpence in earnest of the bear-ward and lead his apes into hell.

Leonato Well then, go you into hell?

Beatrice No, but to the gate, and there will the devil meet me like an old cuckold with horns on his head, and say "Get you to heaven, Beatrice, get you to heaven. Here's no place for you maids." So deliver I up my apes, and away to Saint Peter for the heavens. He shows me where the bachelors sit, and there live we as merry as the day is long.

Antonio *[To Hero.]* Well, niece, I trust you will be ruled by your father.

Beatrice Yes faith, it is my cousin's duty to make curtsy and say, "Father, as it please you." But yet for all that, cousin, let him be a handsome fellow, or else make another curtsy, and say, "Father, as it please me."

SHAKESPEARE'S WORLD

Marriage

Beatrice is against marriage at the start of the play. She hints she has been scorned in love before. In Shakespeare's time, men negotiated marriage for their children (unless a son was old enough to negotiate for himself). Women were legally required to agree to the marriage in the wedding ceremony, but they had less say in whom they married.

In the play, Beatrice is living with her uncle, Leonato. As her closest male relative, Leonato would negotiate the terms of her marriage. In Shakespeare's time, women were defined by their relationship to marriage: as a maid, a wife or a widow. It was difficult for a woman to remain unmarried because she could not inherit land and only lower class women worked. Beatrice would not be able to work. Also, people might question a woman's chastity if she was unmarried, which was bad for her reputation. Leonato wants to marry his niece to a suitable husband to ensure her financial and social security.

23 **Just:** exactly so
26 **the woollen:** rough, scratchy wool blankets
27 **light on:** happen to find
28 **apparel:** clothes
33 **even:** simply
33 **in earnest of:** as advanced payment from
34 **the bear-ward:** the man who looks after the bears used in bear-baiting where dogs attacked bears for an audience
34 **lead his apes into hell:** a proverb said that women who died unmarried had to lead apes into hell
40 **Saint Peter:** the saint who stood at the gates of heaven, deciding who to let in
41 **bachelors:** unmarried men and women

A 2008, *B* 2011.

1. Both photos were taken at the same point in the play. Pick the stage direction or a line that fits this exact moment. Give reasons for your answer.
2. Both directors have added to what is in the text. What have they done, and why do you think they have done it?
3. Find the man with a false beard in Photo B. Why is this character wearing this false beard at this point in the play? Explain your answer. (It may help to look back at other photos from 2011.)

Leonato Well, niece, I hope to see you one day fitted with a husband.

Beatrice Not till God make men of some other metal than earth. Would it not grieve a woman to be overmastered with a piece of valiant dust? To make an account of her life to a clod of wayward marl? No, uncle, I'll none. Adam's sons are my brethren, and truly I hold it a sin to match in my kindred.

Leonato Daughter, remember what I told you. If the Prince do solicit you in that kind, you know your answer.

Beatrice The fault will be in the music cousin, if you be not wooed in good time. If the Prince be too important, tell him there is measure in everything, and so dance out the answer. For hear me, Hero, wooing, wedding, and repenting is as a Scotch jig, a measure, and a cinquepace. The first suit is hot and hasty like a Scotch jig (and full as fantastical), the wedding, mannerly modest (as a measure, full of state and ancientry), and then comes repentance and with his bad legs falls into the cinquepace faster and faster, till he sink into his grave.

Leonato Cousin, you apprehend passing shrewdly.

Beatrice I have a good eye uncle, I can see a church by daylight.

Leonato The revellers are entering brother, make good room.

Enter, masked, Don Pedro, Claudio, Benedick, Balthasar, Don John, Borachio, and other masquers, with a drummer.

Don Pedro *[To Hero.]* Lady, will you walk a bout with your friend? *[The dancing starts.]*

Hero So, you walk softly and look sweetly and say nothing. I am yours for the walk, and especially when I walk away.

Don Pedro With me in your company?

Hero I may say so when I please.

Don Pedro And when please you to say so?

Hero When I like your favour, for God defend the lute should be like the case.

Don Pedro My visor is Philemon's roof, within the house is Jove.

Hero Why then, your visor should be thatched.

Don Pedro Speak low if you speak love.

[They dance to one side. Benedick and Margaret move forward.]

Benedick Well, I would you did like me.

Margaret So would not I for your own sake, for I have many ill qualities.

Benedick Which is one?

Margaret I say my prayers aloud.

51 **metal:** material, substance (the rest of the speech puns on God making Adam from earth – variously dust, clay, marl)
52 **overmastered with:** ruled by
54 **I'll none:** I won't have a husband
55 **match:** marry
58 **solicit you in that kind:** propose marriage
59 **the music:** the rest of the speech puns on wooing and marriage using musical terms
60 **important:** importunate, pushy
61 **measure:** double meaning: 1) a slowish dance; 2) moderation
63 **a Scotch jig, a measure, and a cinquepace:** three kinds of dance
64 **The first suit:** wooing, courtship
65 **full as fantastical:** just as energetic and passionate
66 **state and ancientry:** formality and tradition
69 **passing shrewdly:** far too spitefully (of marriage)
71 **make good room:** let them in
72 **walk a bout:** dance
73 **So, you:** as long as you
78 **favour:** face
78–9 **the lute should be like the case:** your face is as ugly as your mask
80 **Philemon's roof:** plain and poor (referring to the home of a peasant in Roman mythology, who was visited by the god Jove in disguise)
80 **within the house is Jove:** I'm handsome as a god under the mask
81 **visor should be thatched:** mask should have hair
83 **I would:** I wish
84–5 **ill qualities:** bad character traits

A **Ursula and Antonio, 2011.**

What choice has the director made in this production which explains why Ursula knows it is Antonio? Explain your answer.

Helen Weir, John Stahl

B **Beatrice and Benedick, 2008.**

Pick a line from page 29 that you think was being spoken when this photo was taken. Give reasons for your answer.

Kirsty Besterman, Bill Buckhurst

Benedick I love you the better. The hearers may cry Amen.

Margaret God match me with a good dancer.

[Balthasar replaces Benedick.]

Balthasar Amen.

Margaret And God keep him out of my sight when the dance is done. Answer, clerk.

Balthasar No more words, the clerk is answered.

[They dance to one side, Ursula and Antonio move forward.]

Ursula I know you well enough, you are Signor Antonio.

Antonio At a word, I am not.

Ursula I know you by the waggling of your head.

Antonio To tell you true, I counterfeit him.

Ursula You could never do him so ill-well unless you were the very man. Here's his dry hand up and down. You are he, you are he!

Antonio At a word, I am not.

Ursula Come, come, do you think I do not know you by your excellent wit? Can virtue hide itself? Go to, mum, you are he. Graces will appear, and there's an end.

[They dance to one side, Beatrice and Benedick move forward.]

Beatrice Will you not tell me who told you so?

Benedick No, you shall pardon me.

Beatrice Nor will you not tell me who you are?

Benedick Not now.

Beatrice That I was disdainful, and that I had my good wit out of the *Hundred Merry Tales*, well, this was Signor Benedick that said so.

Benedick What's he?

Beatrice I am sure you know him well enough.

Benedick Not I, believe me.

Beatrice Did he never make you laugh?

Benedick I pray you, what is he?

Beatrice Why, he is the Prince's jester, a very dull fool. Only his gift is in devising impossible slanders. None but libertines delight in him, and the commendation is not in his wit, but in his villainy, for he both pleases men and angers them, and then they laugh at him and beat him. I am sure he is in the fleet, I would he had boarded me.

92 **Answer, clerk:** the parish clerk led the responses in the church service

95 **At a word:** in brief

97 **I counterfeit him:** I'm imitating him

98 **do him so ill-well:** impersonate his imperfections so well

99 **dry hand:** wrinkled hand

99 **up and down:** done exactly right

103 **Go to, mum:** give over

104 **there's an end:** that's all there is to it

106 **you shall pardon me:** sorry, I can't do that

110 ***Hundred Merry Tales*:** a pamphlet of jokes and stories, mostly rude and not very clever

116 **what is he:** what's his social position?

117 **jester/fool:** lords often had a jester or fool at court, from a lower social class, to amuse them

117–8 **Only his gift:** the only thing he can do

118 **impossible:** unbelievable

119 **libertines:** people with no morals

119 **the commendation:** the reason they like him

120 **villainy:** coarse humour and rudeness

122 **in the fleet:** one of the dancers

123 **boarded:** tackled – double meaning: 1) in wordplay; 2) sexually

Borachio and Don John, between lines 133 and 146, 2004.

Which is which? Give at least two reasons for your answer.

Gabrielle Reidy, Rachel Sanders

SHAKESPEARE'S WORLD

Gulling

In Shakespeare's time someone who was tricked or 'conned' was often said to be '*gulled*'. The tricked person was a '*gull*'; the process of tricking was '*gulling*'. It is related to the modern English word 'gullible'. 'Gulling' was often used to describe the tricks used by con-men to trick people out of money – usually by playing on their greed. Gulls were seldom innocent. In *Much Ado About Nothing*, Don Pedro's plan to trick Beatrice and Benedick into loving each other is gulling. The scenes in which this happens – Act 2 Scene 3 and Act 3 Scene 1 – are called 'the gulling scenes'. Don John's plot is not gulling: it is too malicious and is tricking the innocent. Gulling is very common in the plays of Shakespeare's time. Characters who are gulled are normally pompous, or firm in their beliefs. The gulling reveals how shallow those beliefs can be.

Gulling creates a situation where the audience know more than some of the characters on the stage. This situation is called dramatic irony. Dramatic irony is important for comic effect in gulling scenes. We need to know that Benedick is being tricked so that we can laugh at him, especially when he says things such as 'This can be no trick' (Act 2 Scene 3, line 199). This line of Benedick's is typical of gulls. When they have been duped, they very often claim that there is no possibility that it is a trick.

Gulling is common in comedies, but is too light-hearted for tragedies, even tragedies which have comic characters. One of Shakespeare's most notable gulls, however, is in a history play. Sir John Falstaff is the victim of an elaborate practical joke in *The First Part of Henry IV*. The same character is also gulled in *The Merry Wives of Windsor*.

Benedick When I know the gentleman, I'll tell him what you say.

Beatrice Do, do. He'll but break a comparison or two on me, which peradventure (not marked or not laughed at), strikes him into melancholy, and then there's a partridge wing saved, for the fool will eat no supper that night. We must follow the leaders.

Benedick In every good thing.

Beatrice Nay, if they lead to any ill, I will leave them at the next turning.

Music for a new dance, all exit dancing, except Don John, Borachio, and Claudio.

Don John Sure my brother is amorous on Hero, and hath withdrawn her father to break with him about it. The ladies follow her, and but one visor remains.

Borachio And that is Claudio, I know him by his bearing.

Don John *[To Claudio.]* Are you not Signor Benedick?

Claudio You know me well, I am he.

Don John Signor, you are very near my brother in his love. He is enamoured on Hero. I pray you dissuade him from her, she is no equal for his birth. You may do the part of an honest man in it.

Claudio How know you he loves her?

Don John I heard him swear his affection.

Borachio So did I too, and he swore he would marry her tonight.

Don John Come, let us to the banquet.

Exit Don John and Borachio.

Claudio
Thus answer I in name of Benedick,
But hear these ill news with the ears of Claudio.
'Tis certain so, the Prince woos for himself.
Friendship is constant in all other things
Save in the office and affairs of love.
Therefore all hearts in love use their own tongues.
Let every eye negotiate for itself,
And trust no agent. For beauty is a witch
Against whose charms faith melteth into blood.
This is an accident of hourly proof,
Which I mistrusted not. Farewell therefore Hero.

Enter Benedick.

Benedick Count Claudio?

Claudio Yea, the same.

Benedick Come, will you go with me?

Claudio Wither?

---

124 **I know:** I'm introduced to
125 **break a comparison:** make a rude remark
126 **peradventure:** perhaps
129 **follow the leaders:** keep up in the dance
133 **amorous on:** in love with
134 **withdrawn:** taken aside
135 **visor:** masked person
136 **his bearing:** the way he moves
139 **very near my brother in his love:** a close friend of my brother
140 **enamoured on:** in love with
141 **no equal for his birth:** of too low a social status
146 **the banquet:** the wine and sweets served at the end of a feast like this
150 **constant:** loyal
151 **Save:** except for
151 **the office and affairs:** the business
152 **use their:** should use their
154 **trust no agent:** don't trust anyone to do your courtship for you
155 **faith:** loyalty
155 **into blood:** passion
156 **an accident of hourly proof:** something that happens all the time
157 **I mistrusted not:** I didn't suspect
161 **Wither?:** where?

Don John and Benedick, 2011.

1. Benedick is speaking. What does his body language suggest about his attitude? Explain your answer.
2. Benedick has four speeches on page 33 after Don Pedro enters. Which fits best with the body language in the photo? Give reasons for your answer.
3. The photographer was standing right by the back of the stage, and the actors are right at the front of the stage. Why might the director have staged it like this? Give reasons for your answer.

Mathew Pidgeon, Charles Edwards

Actor's view

Bill Buckhurst
Benedick, 2008

What's happened is he's seen Don Pedro chatting to Hero and we learn a lot about this guy. He runs out and the first thing he says, he sees Claudio and goes, 'Hey listen! The Prince hath got your Hero. Come will you go with me?' And that shows a great loyalty to Claudio. He's concerned about his mate, and Claudio's a very close mate of his, and he's basically saying, 'come on, come and sort it out. This is the girl you like.' Even though, in the scene before, he's been mocking him about it, actually he clearly does care about Claudio and the fact that he likes this girl because he comes and tells him. He says, 'Look, you know, if you like her, don't lose her.' Because Don Pedro is talking to her and obviously Benedick doesn't know that it's completely innocent, that there's nothing going on. So I think that we learn from his relationship with Claudio, even though he joshes with him, like he has done in the first scene, [that] he does care about him and he's actively encouraging Claudio to go and claim her for himself. Then Don Pedro arrives and he very cleverly attacks Don Pedro in quite a poetic way really, saying, 'I've found Claudio, he's as melancholy as a school boy...' Which is basically wrapping up in a nice way, 'you've been chatting up Hero and that's really out of order!' So we also learn there that he has a relationship with his boss, where he feels comfortable to bring him up on things.

Benedick Even to the next willow, about your own business, Count. What fashion will you wear the garland of? About your neck, like an usurer's chain? Or under your arm, like a lieutenant's scarf? You must wear it one way, for the Prince hath got your Hero.

Claudio I wish him joy of her.

Benedick Why, that's spoken like an honest drover, so they sell bullocks. But did you think the Prince would have served you thus?

Claudio I pray you leave me.

Benedick Ho! now you strike like the blind man, 'twas the boy that stole your meat, and you'll beat the post.

Claudio If it will not be, I'll leave you. *Exit Claudio.*

Benedick Alas, poor hurt fowl, now will he creep into sedges. But that my Lady Beatrice should know me, and not know me. The Prince's fool! Ha! It may be I go under that title because I am merry. Yea, but so I am apt to do myself wrong. I am not so reputed, it is the base (though bitter) disposition of Beatrice, that puts the world into her person and so gives me out. Well, I'll be revenged as I may.

Enter Don Pedro, Hero, and Leonato.

Don Pedro Now signor, where's the Count? Did you see him?

Benedick Troth my lord, I have played the part of Lady Fame, I found him here as melancholy as a lodge in a warren. I told him, and I think I told him true, that your grace had got the good will of this young lady, and I offered him my company to a willow tree, either to make him a garland, as being forsaken, or to bind him up a rod, as being worthy to be whipped.

Don Pedro To be whipped? What's his fault?

Benedick The flat transgression of a schoolboy, who being overjoyed with finding a bird's nest, shows it his companion, and he steals it.

Don Pedro Wilt thou make a trust a transgression? The transgression is in the stealer.

Benedick Yet it had not been amiss the rod had been made, and the garland too, for the garland he might have worn himself, and the rod he might have bestowed on you, who (as I take it) have stolen his bird's nest.

Don Pedro I will but teach them to sing, and restore them to the owner.

Benedick If their singing answer your saying, by my faith you say honestly.

Don Pedro The Lady Beatrice hath a quarrel to you. The gentleman that danced with her told her she is much wronged by you.

162 **willow:** symbol of lovers whose love is not returned
163 **What fashion will you … garland of?:** How will you wear you willow garland?
164 **usurer's chain:** money-lender's gold necklace
168 **drover:** cattle dealer
168 **so:** this is how
170 **served you thus:** done such a thing to you
172 **strike like the blind man:** hit out at the wrong target
174 **If it will not be:** if you won't go
175 **hurt fowl:** injured bird
175 **sedges:** rough grass where a wounded bird might hide from predators
176 **But that:** what a surprise that
178 **but so am I apt to:** but if I think like that I'm likely to
179 **base:** unworthy
180–1 **puts the world into her person:** assumes everyone thinks like her
184 **Lady Fame:** gossip personified
185 **a lodge in a warren:** an isolated house in fenced off parkland
192 **flat transgression:** simple wrongdoing
193 **bird's nest:** meaning Hero
195 **a trust:** trusting someone
199 **bestowed on:** given
203 **If their singing answer your saying:** if that's the case (that he's really wooed her for Claudio)

Claudio (in the foreground), Beatrice, Don Pedro, Leonato and Hero, 2011.

1 Which line could be used as a caption for this photo? Explain your answer.

2 How has the director used the staging to emphasise Claudio's state of mind?

Philip Cumbus, Eve Best, Ewan Stewart, Joseph Marcell, Ony Uhiara

FROM THE REHEARSAL ROOM...

LOVE ON THE LINE

This is a repeat of the activity on page 10. Look back to remind yourself of the instructions.

- Discuss what Benedick says about Beatrice.

1 Where is Benedick on the line? Quote from the text to support your answer.

- Discuss what Beatrice says about Benedick.

2 Where is Beatrice on the line? Quote from the text to support your answer.

- Stand in the places on the line, and compare your answers with other groups. Use your quotes to support your views.

3 Record your answers, and the ones that the majority of the class agree on.

FROM THE REHEARSAL ROOM...

EXPRESSING FEELINGS

Nominate as many people to do this activity as there is space for.

- Read Benedick's speech (lines 207–227).
  - Read the speech aloud while walking around.
  - Each time you get to a punctuation mark, change direction and carry on walking.
- Read the speech again. This time, change direction every time Benedick compares Beatrice to something else.

1 What does the speech reveal about Benedick's state of mind after his exchange with Beatrice at the ball?

2 What do the type of comparisons tell us about how Benedick feels about Beatrice?

Benedick O, she misused me past the endurance of a block. An oak but with one green leaf on it would have answered her. My very visor began to assume life and scold with her. She told me, not thinking I had been myself, that I was the Prince's jester, that I was duller than a great thaw, huddling jest upon jest with such impossible conveyance upon me, that I stood like a man at a mark, with a whole army shooting at me. She speaks poniards, and every word stabs. If her breath were as terrible as her terminations, there were no living near her, she would infect to the North Star. I would not marry her, though she were endowed with all that Adam had left him before he transgressed. She would have made Hercules have turned spit, yea, and have cleft his club to make the fire too. Come, talk not of her. You shall find her the infernal Ate in good apparel. I would to God some scholar would conjure her, for certainly while she is here, a man may live as quiet in hell as in a sanctuary, and people sin upon purpose, because they would go thither. So indeed all disquiet, horror, and perturbation follows her.

Enter Claudio, Beatrice, Leonato, and Hero.

Don Pedro Look, here she comes.

Benedick Will your grace command me any service to the world's end? I will go on the slightest errand now to the Antipodes that you can devise to send me on. I will fetch you a tooth-picker now from the furthest inch of Asia, bring you the length of Prester John's foot, fetch you a hair off the great Cham's beard, do you any embassage to the Pygmies, rather than hold three words' conference with this harpy. You have no employment for me?

Don Pedro None, but to desire your good company.

Benedick O God sir, here's a dish I love not, I cannot endure my Lady Tongue. *He exits.*

Don Pedro Come lady, come, you have lost the heart of Signor Benedick.

Beatrice Indeed my lord, he lent it me awhile, and I gave him use for it, a double heart for his single one. Marry, once before he won it of me, with false dice, therefore your Grace may well say I have lost it.

Don Pedro You have put him down lady, you have put him down.

Beatrice So I would not he should do me, my lord, lest I should prove the mother of fools. I have brought Count Claudio, whom you sent me to seek.

Don Pedro Why, how now Count? Wherefore are you sad?

Claudio Not sad, my lord.

Don Pedro How then? Sick?

---

207 **misused:** abused
207 **past the endurance of a block:** more than even a block of wood could stand
208 **but with:** with only
209 **My very visor:** even my mask
209 **assume life:** come to life
211–2 **great thaw:** when the snows of winter melted and roads were too muddy to travel easily so people stayed at home
212–3 **impossible conveyance:** skilful generalship (start of a run of army images)
213 **at a mark:** fixed to a target
214 **poniards:** daggers
216 **terminations:** words; conclusions (about me)
218–9 **all that Adam ... he transgressed:** the Garden of Eden
220 **turned spit:** do the most unpleasant kitchen work, turning the roasting spit over the fire
220 **cleft:** split (here, for firewood)
222 **infernal Ate:** a goddess of infatuation, rash actions and discord
223 **some scholar would conjure her:** a clever man who knows Latin would say the spell to send her to hell
224–5 **as quiet in hell as in a sanctuary:** hell's as quiet as a holy retreat
226 **thither:** there [to hell]
230–1 **the Antipodes:** the other side of the world
231 **devise:** invent
233 **Prester John:** the legendary ruler of an Eastern kingdom
234 **the Great Cham:** emperor of China
235 **Pygmies:** a race of very small people thought at the time to live in Asia
236 **harpy:** fierce, cruel mythical creature, birdlike, with the head of a woman
245 **false dice:** meaning false promises
248 **So I would not he should do me:** I don't want him to put me down (sexual meaning)
251 **Wherefore:** why

FROM THE REHEARSAL ROOM...

IS HE FOR REAL?

In groups, read Don Pedro's proposal (lines 278–295). Is his proposal serious or just banter? What different ways could Beatrice react to it?

- Explore different ways of playing this section, including one where he is serious, and one where he isn't. Pick the one you prefer.
- Watch other pairs' interpretations.

1 Which version do you think was the most effective? Explain why.

2 Look again at lines 290–295. Is Beatrice's refusal going to be a problem with Don Pedro in the future? Quote from the text to support your answer.

3 How would you direct the scene?

SHAKESPEARE'S WORLD

Betrothal

A betrothal was a formal commitment between a man and woman to marry. While a betrothal wasn't as binding as marriage, it was a formal contract. Sometimes betrothals were marked with ceremonies, including exchanging vows and rings. If there was no ceremony, the families announced the betrothal publicly. Betrothals were much more serious than an engagement today. Some couples regarded being betrothed as the same as being married. Breaking off a betrothal was seen as very wrong. It could ruin the reputation of the person who broke off the betrothal, and the person they were betrothed to. It could also make it harder for both people to arrange another marriage.

Beatrice and Don Pedro during his proposal (lines 278–295), 2011.

1 Which photo was taken earlier in the scene? Give reasons for your answer.

2 On the evidence of these photos, did the director of the 2011 production choose to play Don Pedro's proposal as serious, or as a joke? Explain your answer.

Eve Best, Ewan Stewart

Claudio Neither, my Lord.

Beatrice The Count is neither sad, nor sick, nor merry, nor well, but civil count, civil as an orange, and something of that jealous complexion.

Don Pedro I' faith lady, I think your blazon to be true, though I'll be sworn, if he be so, his conceit is false. Here Claudio, I have wooed in thy name, and fair Hero is won. I have broke with her father, and his good will obtained. Name the day of marriage, and God give thee joy!

Leonato Count, take of me my daughter, and with her my fortunes. His Grace hath made the match, and all grace say "Amen" to it.

Beatrice Speak Count, 'tis your cue.

Claudio Silence is the perfectest herald of joy, I were but little happy if I could say how much. Lady, as you are mine, I am yours. I give away myself for you and dote upon the exchange.

overwhelmed, romantic talks like a poet, promises her to be hers forever can't handle the situation, don't know what to say convinced about love

Beatrice Speak cousin, or (if you cannot), stop his mouth with a kiss and let not him speak neither.

Don Pedro In faith lady, you have a merry heart.

Beatrice Yea my lord, I thank it, poor fool, it keeps on the windy side of care. My cousin tells him in his ear that he is in her heart.

Claudio And so she doth, cousin.

Beatrice Good Lord for alliance! Thus goes every one to the world but I, and I am sunburnt. I may sit in a corner and cry "Heigh-ho for a husband!"

Don Pedro Lady Beatrice, I will get you one.

Beatrice I would rather have one of your father's getting. Hath your Grace ne'er a brother like you? Your father got excellent husbands, if a maid could come by them.

Don Pedro Will you have me, lady?

Beatrice No, my lord, unless I might have another for working days. Your Grace is too costly to wear every day. But I beseech your Grace pardon me. I was born to speak all mirth and no matter.

Don Pedro Your silence most offends me, and to be merry best becomes you, for out of question you were born in a merry hour.

Beatrice No, sure my lord, my mother cried, but then there was a star danced, and under that was I born. Cousins, God give you joy!

Leonato Niece, will you look to those things I told you of?

Beatrice I cry you mercy uncle. – By your Grace's pardon.

256 **civil:** used in the next lines to pun on Seville oranges, which are very bitter
258 **blazon:** description
259 **conceit:** view of the situation
261 **broke:** negotiated
264–5 **all grace say "Amen" to it:** may God approve it
267 **herald:** demonstration
267–8 **I were but little happy ... say how much:** I'd be able to describe my happiness only if it was less than it is
274–5 **the windy side of care:** safe (downwind) from sorrow

superficial

278 **Good Lord for alliance!**: Thank God for marriage!
279 **sunburnt**: unattractive (dark skin, tanned or natural, was seen as very unattractive)
282 **getting**: fathering
288–9 **I was born to speak ... no matter**: I can't help making a joke of everything
291 **becomes**: suits
291 **out of question**: undoubtedly
293 **cried**: from the pain of giving birth
294 **under that was I born**: that made me a merry person
297 **I cry you mercy**: sorry
297 **By your Grace's pardon**: excuse me, Count, I must go

Leonato, Don Pedro, Hero, Claudio, 2008.

1 At which point towards the end of the scene do you think this photo was taken? Give reasons for your answer.

2 Why are the characters dressed as they are? Explain your answer.

Christopher John Hall, Tom Davey, Natasha Magigi, Navin Chowdhry

Actor's view

Ewan Stewart
Don Pedro, 2011

Where I am at the moment with Don Pedro is that he's quite manipulative, he sets up these things with Beatrice and Benedick. He sets that up, and he sets up Claudio and Hero, so he's somebody who likes to work behind the scenes. And then I sense maybe operating from a place where, in some ways, [he is] manipulating these other people, but not really [involving] himself. He has a go to set himself up with Beatrice at one point, and that doesn't work out, but mostly you see him as passive-aggressive, but emotionally [uninvolved]. I think you take these things on board and look at them for a while in rehearsal, then sort of let them go onto a very, very backburner.

Director's Note, 2.1

- The men enter the dance disguised in masks.
- Beatrice pretends not to recognise Benedick and mocks him.
- Don John convinces Claudio that Don Pedro has double-crossed him, and wants Hero for himself.
- Claudio sulks.
- Eventually Claudio goes to Don Pedro, finds out he has not been double-crossed, and that Don Pedro has fixed things for Hero to marry him.
- Leonato fixes the wedding for seven days time, and Don Pedro plans to use the time by tricking Beatrice and Benedick into falling in love.
- Mistakes and misunderstandings are a big part of this play. How many are there in this scene?

Exit Beatrice.

Don Pedro By my troth, a pleasant-spirited lady.

Leonato There's little of the melancholy element in her my lord. She is never sad but when she sleeps, and not ever sad then, for I have heard my daughter say she hath often dreamt of unhappiness and waked herself with laughing.

Don Pedro She cannot endure to hear tell of a husband.

Leonato O, by no means. She mocks all her wooers out of suit.

Don Pedro She were an excellent wife for Benedick.

Leonato O Lord, my lord, if they were but a week married, they would talk themselves mad.

Don Pedro Count Claudio, when mean you to go to church?

Claudio Tomorrow, my lord, time goes on crutches till love have all his rites.

Leonato Not till Monday, my dear son, which is hence a just seven-night, and a time too brief too, to have all things answer my mind.

Don Pedro Come, you shake the head at so long a breathing, but I warrant thee Claudio, the time shall not go dully by us. I will in the interim undertake one of Hercules' labours, which is, to bring Signor Benedick and the Lady Beatrice into a mountain of affection, th' one with th' other. I would fain have it a match, and I doubt not but to fashion it, if you three will but minister such assistance as I shall give you direction.

Leonato My lord, I am for you, though it cost me ten nights' watchings.

Claudio And I my lord.

Don Pedro And you too, gentle Hero?

Hero I will do any modest office, my lord, to help my cousin to a good husband.

Don Pedro And Benedick is not the unhopefullest husband that I know. Thus far can I praise him, he is of a noble strain, of approved valour, and confirmed honesty. I will teach you how to humour your cousin, that she shall fall in love with Benedick. — And I, with your two helps, will so practice on Benedick that, in despite of his quick wit and his queasy stomach, he shall fall in love with Beatrice. If we can do this, Cupid is no longer an archer. His glory shall be ours, for we are the only love-gods. Go in with me, and I will tell you my drift.

Exit all.

characterisengen
development
constellation

---

299 **the melancholy element:** sadness
300 **sad:** this meant both sad and serious
300 **ever:** always
304 **out of suit:** until they give up wooing
305 **were:** would be
308 **to go to church:** to marry
309 **goes on crutches:** limps along
310 **all his rites:** when Claudio and Hero consummate their marriage
311 **hence:** from here
311–2 **a just seven-night:** exactly a week
313 **answer my mind:** just as I want them
314 **breathing:** pause, delay
315 **I warrant thee:** I promise
316 **interim:** meantime
319 **I would fain have it a match:** I'd like them to marry
319–20 **I doubt not but to fashion it:** I'm sure I can make it happen
320 **minister:** give
321 **give you direction:** tell you
322 **I am for you:** I'll follow you
323 **watchings:** of staying awake
326 **modest office:** task suitable for my sex and status
328 **unhopefullest:** most unsuitable
329 **strain:** ancestry, family
330 **of approved valour:** known to be brave
330 **confirmed honesty:** known to be honourable
332 **your two helps:** your help (to Leonato and Claudio)
333 **practice on:** trick
334 **his queasy stomach:** the fact he says the thought of marriage makes him sick
337 **my drift:** what I intend to do

Borachio and Don John, 2011.

1 Which character is from the higher social class? How does the production show this?
2 Which character is taking the lead in the discussion? How does the production show this?

Joe Caffrey, Matthew Pidgeon

FROM THE REHEARSAL ROOM...

THE MAN AND THE PLAN

In pairs, face each other and read aloud the conversation between Don John and Borachio in the *Working Cut*.

- Now read the extract again, but whisper each line.
- Which words stand out? Discuss what they reveal about Don John's character.

1 How would you describe Don John?

2 What words does he use that tell us about what type of man he is?

- In small groups, read Borachio's plan and make a series of freeze frames that show each stage of the plan. Give each frame a caption from the text.

3 Explain which lines and words were important to you in the creation of each of the frames.

Working Cut – text for experiment

Don John Any bar, any cross, any impediment will be medicinable to me. I am sick in displeasure to him. How canst thou cross this marriage?

Borachio I am in the favour of Margaret, the waiting gentlewoman to Hero. I can, at any unseasonable instant of the night, appoint her to look out at her lady's chamber window.

Don John What life is in that to be the death of this marriage?

Borachio Go you to the Prince your brother, tell him that he hath wronged his honour in marrying the renowned Claudio, to a contaminated stale, such a one as Hero.

Don John What proof shall I make of that?

Borachio Proof enough to misuse the Prince, to vex Claudio, to undo Hero, and kill Leonato.

Don John Only to despite them, I will endeavour anything.

ACT 2 SCENE 2

Enter Don John and Borachio.

Don John It is so. The Count Claudio shall marry the daughter of Leonato.

Borachio Yea, my lord, but I can cross it.

Don John Any bar, any cross, any impediment will be medicinable to me. I am sick in displeasure to him, and whatsoever comes athwart his affection ranges evenly with mine. How canst thou cross this marriage?

Borachio Not honestly my lord, but so covertly that no dishonesty shall appear in me.

Don John Show me briefly how.

Borachio I think I told your lordship a year since, how much I am in the favour of Margaret, the waiting gentlewoman to Hero.

Don John I remember.

Borachio I can, at any unseasonable instant of the night, appoint her to look out at her lady's chamber window.

Don John What life is in that to be the death of this marriage?

Borachio The poison of that lies in you to temper. Go you to the Prince your brother, spare not to tell him that he hath wronged his honour in marrying the renowned Claudio, whose estimation do you mightily hold up, to a contaminated stale, such a one as Hero.

Don John What proof shall I make of that?

Borachio Proof enough to misuse the Prince, to vex Claudio, to undo Hero, and kill Leonato. Look you for any other issue?

Don John Only to despite them, I will endeavour anything.

Borachio Go then, find a meet hour to draw Don Pedro and the Count Claudio alone. Tell them that you know that Hero loves me. Intend a kind of zeal both to the Prince and Claudio (as in love of your brother's honour, who hath made this match, and his friend's reputation, who is thus like to be cozened with the semblance of a maid), that you have discovered thus. They will scarcely believe this without trial. Offer them instances, which shall bear no less likelihood than to see me at her chamber window, hear me call Margaret "Hero", hear Margaret term me "Claudio". And bring them to see this the very night before the intended wedding (for in the meantime I will so fashion the matter that Hero shall be absent), and there shall appear such seeming truth of Hero's disloyalty that jealousy shall be called assurance, and all the preparation overthrown.

3 **cross it:** get it cancelled
4 **bar:** legal objection
4 **impediment:** obstruction
5 **medicinable to me:** make me feel better
5 **I am sick in displeasure to him:** I dislike him so much it makes me feel ill
6–7 **whatsoever comes athwart ... evenly with mine:** whatever stops him getting what he wants is what I want to happen
8 **covertly:** secretly
11 **since:** ago
15 **unseasonable instant:** inappropriate time
17 **What life is in that to be:** how will that be
18 **lies in you to temper:** you can mix up
19 **spare not to tell him:** tell him frankly
21 **estimation:** reputation
21 **do you mightily hold up:** you must exaggerate
22 **contaminated stale:** diseased whore
24 **misuse:** deceive
24 **vex:** torment
24 **undo:** ruin the reputation of
25 **issue:** result
26 **Only to despite them:** as long as it hurts them
27 **meet:** suitable
29 **Intend:** pretend
29 **zeal:** loyalty
32 **cozened:** tricked
32–3 **the semblance of a maid:** one who only pretends to be a virgin
33 **that you have discovered thus:** that you have told them
34 **trial:** asking for evidence
34 **instances:** evidence
35 **which shall bear no less likelihood:** what better than
39 **I will so fashion the matter:** I'll make sure
41 **disloyalty:** infidelity
41 **jealousy:** suspicion
42 **assurance:** certainty
42 **preparation:** for the wedding

Don John Grow this to what adverse issue it can, I will put it in practice. Be cunning in the working this, and thy fee is a thousand ducats.

Borachio Be you constant in the accusation, and my cunning shall not shame me.

Don John I will presently go learn their day of marriage.

Exit both.

43 **Grow this to what adverse issue it can:** whatever evil comes of this
46 **Be you constant in the accusation:** stick to your story
48 **presently:** now

Director's Note, 2.2

- ✔ Borachio comes up with a plan for Don John to wreck the marriage.
- ✔ Borachio will get Margaret to dress in Hero's clothes, and Don John will arrange for Claudio to see Borachio and Margaret together, so he will mistake Margaret for Hero.
- ✔ Claudio will believe Hero is unfaithful, and will call off the wedding.
- ✔ How important is this mistake?

ACT 2 SCENE 3

Enter Benedick alone.

Benedick Boy!

[Enter Boy.]

Boy Signor.

Benedick In my chamber window lies a book. Bring it hither to me in the orchard.

Boy I am here already sir.

Benedick I know that, but I would have thee hence and here again. *Exit Boy.*
I do much wonder that one man, seeing how much another man is a fool when he dedicates his behaviours to love, will, after he hath laughed at such shallow follies in others, become the argument of his own scorn by falling in love. And such a man is Claudio. I have known when there was no music with him but the drum and the fife, and now had he rather hear the tabor and the pipe. I have known when he would have walked ten mile afoot to see a good armour, and now will he lie ten nights awake carving the fashion of a new doublet. He was wont to speak plain and to the

3 **hither:** here
5 **I am here already:** I'll be quick as a flash (Benedick pretends to misunderstand)
9–10 **dedicates his behaviours to love:** acts the lover
11 **argument:** subject
14 **the drum and the fife:** the music of war
14–5 **the tabor and the pipe:** the music of domestic life
17–8 **carving the fashion of a new doublet:** designing a new jacket
18 **He was wont to:** he used to

music - metaphors

FROM THE REHEARSAL ROOM...

MONOLOGUE AS DUOLOGUE

Act 2 Scene 3 opens with Benedick sharing his thoughts with the audience.

- In pairs, read most of Benedick's soliloquy (lines 8–35) as a duologue. Each time you get to a full stop, question mark or exclamation mark, change reader until the next punctuation mark. Continue this pattern to line 35.

1 What does Benedick think of Claudio's changed behaviour?

2 Describe Benedick's attitude towards the effect marriage can have on people.

- Re-read lines 26–35, still changing reader at the end of each sentence.

3 List the qualities and attributes in a woman that would make Benedick consider marriage.

4 What is his attitude to marriage at this stage of the play?

purpose (like an honest man and a soldier), and now is he turned orthography, his words are a very fantastical banquet, just so many strange dishes. May I be so converted and see with these eyes? I cannot tell, I think not. I will not be sworn, but love may transform me to an oyster, but I'll take my oath on it, till he have made an oyster of me, he shall never make me such a fool. One woman is fair, yet I am well. Another is wise, yet I am well. Another virtuous, yet I am well. But till all graces be in one woman, one woman shall not come in my grace. Rich she shall be, that's certain. Wise, or I'll none. Virtuous, or I'll never cheapen her. Fair, or I'll never look on her. Mild, or come not near me. Noble, or not I for an angel. Of good discourse, an excellent musician, and her hair shall be of what colour it please God. Hah! The Prince and Monsieur Love, I will hide me in the arbour. *[He hides.]*

Enter Don Pedro, Leonato, Claudio, and Balthasar.

Don Pedro Come, shall we hear this music?

Claudio Yea my good lord. How still the evening is,
As hushed on purpose to grace harmony.

Don Pedro *[Aside.]* See you where Benedick hath hid himself?

Claudio *[Aside.]* O, very well, my lord. The music ended,
We'll fit the kid-fox with a pennyworth.

Don Pedro Come, Balthasar, we'll hear that song again.

Balthasar O good my lord, tax not so bad a voice
To slander music any more than once.

Don Pedro It is the witness still of excellency
To put a strange face on his own perfection.
I pray thee sing, and let me woo no more.

Balthasar Because you talk of wooing, I will sing,
Since many a wooer doth commence his suit
To her he thinks not worthy, yet he woos,
Yet he will swear he loves.

Don Pedro Nay, pray thee, come,
Or if thou wilt hold no longer argument,
Do it in notes.

Balthasar Note this before my notes,
There's not a note of mine that's worth noting.

Don Pedro Why, these are very crotchets that he speaks,
Note notes forsooth, and nothing.

[Balthasar starts to play.]

Benedick *[Aside.]* Now, divine air! Now is his soul ravished. Is it not strange that sheeps' guts should hale souls out of men's bodies? Well, a horn for my money, when all's done.

Balthasar sings.

19–20 **is he turned orthography:** he's eaten a dictionary
20 **fantastical:** fanciful
21–2 **May I be so converted … with these eyes?:** will I ever change like that?
24 **an oyster:** a totally silent creature (the opposite of Benedick now)
29 **my grace:** my good opinion
30 **cheapen:** bid for her
31–2 **Noble, or not I for an angel:** she has to come from a good family; I won't marry a woman just because she's rich
32 **Of good discourse:** good at making conversation
38 **As:** as if
41 **fit the kid-fox with a pennyworth:** give him more than he bargained for
43 **tax not:** don't make
45 **the witness still:** always a sign of
46 **put a strange face on his own perfection:** to run himself down
47 **let me woo no more:** don't make me keep asking you
49 **doth commence his suit:** begins wooing
53 **Do it in notes:** the start of a run of musical puns
57 **air:** music
58 **hale:** haul, drag
59 **a horn for my money:** I prefer a trumpet (more war-like)

Benedick (background), Leonato, Claudio, Don Pedro, 2011.

What feature of the Globe stage, which Shakespeare would have been very familiar with, has the director used at this point?

Charles Edwards, Joseph Marcell, Philip Cumbus, Ewan Stewart

A

Sigh no more, ladies, sigh no more,
Men were deceivers ever,
One foot in sea and one on shore,
To one thing constant never.
Then sigh not so, but let them go,
And be you blithe and bonny,
Converting all your sounds of woe
Into "Hey, nonny nonny."

Sing no more ditties, sing no moe,
Of dumps so dull and heavy,
The fraud of men was ever so,
Since summer first was leavy.
Then sigh not so, but let them go,
And be you blithe and bonny,
Converting all your sounds of woe
Into "Hey, nonny nonny."

Don Pedro By my troth, a good song.

Balthasar And an ill singer, my lord.

Don Pedro Ha? No, no faith, thou sing'st well enough for a shift.

Benedick *[Aside.]* An he had been a dog that should have howled thus, they would have hanged him. And I pray God his bad voice bode no mischief. I had as lief have heard the night-raven, come what plague could have come after it.

Don Pedro Yea, marry, dost thou hear Balthasar? I pray thee get us some excellent music, for tomorrow night we would have it at the Lady Hero's chamber window.

Balthasar The best I can, my lord.

Don Pedro Do so. Farewell. *Exit Balthasar.*
Come hither Leonato. What was it you told me of today, that your niece Beatrice was in love with Signor Benedick?

Claudio *[To Don Pedro and Leonato.]* O ay, stalk on, stalk on, the fowl sits. — I did never think that lady would have loved any man.

Leonato No, nor I neither. But most wonderful that she should so dote on Signor Benedick, whom she hath in all outward behaviours seemed ever to abhor.

Benedick *[Aside]* Is't possible? Sits the wind in that corner?

Leonato By my troth my lord, I cannot tell what to think of it, but that she loves him with an enraged affection. It is past the infinite of thought.

Don Pedro May be she doth but counterfeit.

Claudio Faith, like enough.

Leonato O God! Counterfeit? There was never counterfeit of passion came so near the life of passion as she discovers it.

Don Pedro Why, what effects of passion shows she?

Claudio *[To Don Pedro and Leonato.]* Bait the hook well, this fish will bite.

65 ***blithe and bonny***: happy and lovely
68 ***ditties***: songs
68 ***moe***: more
69 ***dumps***: sadness; sad songs
71 ***leavy***: leafy
78 **for a shift:** for our needs
79 **An:** if
81 **bode no mischief:** doesn't foretell trouble
81 **I had as lief:** I would rather
82 **night-raven:** a bird whose call foretold disaster, sickness or death
90–1 **stalk on, stalk on, the fowl sits:** keep creeping up on the bird you are hunting (Benedick), I can see him
92 **wonderful:** astonishing
93 **so dote on:** love so excessively
94 **abhor:** hate
95 **Sits the wind in that corner?:** is that the way things are?
97 **enraged affection:** furiously passionate love
98 **past the infinite of thought:** beyond belief
99 **she doth but counterfeit:** she's just pretending
102 **discovers:** displays

Benedick, hiding during this scene:
***B* 2004, *C* 2008.**

Study all four photos A–D on pages 44, 46 and 48.
There is one each from the productions of 2004 and 2008, and two from the production of 2011.

1. Explain at least two similarities in the way the directors of each of these productions have staged this scene.
2. Explain at least two differences in the way the directors of each of these productions have staged this scene.
3. Claudio is speaking in Photo D. At which point in the scene do you think this photo was taken? Give a line number (or numbers) and explain the reasons for your choice.

B Josie Lawrence
C Bill Buckhurst

Leonato What effects my lord? She will sit you — you heard my daughter tell you how.

Claudio She did indeed.

Don Pedro How, how, I pray you? You amaze me. I would have thought her spirit had been invincible against all assaults of affection.

Leonato I would have sworn it had, my lord, especially against Benedick.

Benedick *[Aside.]* I should think this a gull, but that the white-bearded fellow speaks it. Knavery cannot, sure, hide himself in such reverence.

Claudio *[To Don Pedro and Leonato.]* He hath ta'en th' infection. Hold it up.

Don Pedro Hath she made her affection known to Benedick?

Leonato No, and swears she never will. That's her torment.

Claudio 'Tis true indeed, so your daughter says. "Shall I," says she, "that have so oft encountered him with scorn, write to him that I love him?"

Leonato This says she now when she is beginning to write to him, for she'll be up twenty times a night, and there will she sit in her smock till she have writ a sheet of paper. My daughter tells us all.

Claudio Now you talk of a sheet of paper, I remember a pretty jest your daughter told us of.

Leonato O, when she had writ it, and was reading it over, she found Benedick and Beatrice between the sheet?

Claudio That.

Leonato O she tore the letter into a thousand halfpence, railed at herself that she should be so immodest to write to one that she knew would flout her. "I measure him," says she, "by my own spirit, for I should flout him if he writ to me, yea though I love him, I should."

Claudio Then down upon her knees she falls, weeps, sobs, beats her heart, tears her hair, prays, curses. "O sweet Benedick! God give me patience!"

Ben should feel pitty feel sympathy

Leonato She doth indeed, my daughter says so. And the ecstasy hath so much overborne her that my daughter is sometime afeard she will do a desperate outrage to herself. It is very true.

Don Pedro It were good that Benedick knew of it by some other, if she will not discover it.

Claudio To what end? He would make but a sport of it and torment the poor lady worse.

Don Pedro And he should, it were an alms to hang him. She's an excellent sweet lady, and (out of all suspicion), she is virtuous.

---

105 **sit you – you:** Leonato runs out of ideas and hands over to Claudio

113 **a gull:** a trick (see page 30)

114 **Knavery:** trickery

115 **reverence:** a respectable old man

116 **ta'en th' infection:** he's caught (the disease)

116 **Hold it up:** keep the trick going

124 **smock:** undergarment worn as both nightdress and under clothes in the day

129 **between the sheet:** referring to paper, but also to bedsheets

131 **a thousand halfpence:** tiny pieces

131 **railed at:** scolded

133 **flout:** mock

139 **ecstasy:** passion

140 **overborne:** overwhelmed

141–2 **do a desperate outrage to herself:** kill herself

143 **by some other:** from someone else

144 **discover:** tell

145 **To what end?:** what for?

145 **sport:** game

147 **And he should:** if he did

147 **an alms:** an act of charity

148 **(out of all suspicion):** undoubtedly

Benedick (hiding), Don Pedro, Claudio, Leonato, 2011.

Charles Edwards, Ewan Stewart, Philip Cumbus, Joseph Marcell

Claudio And she is exceeding wise.

Don Pedro In everything, but in loving Benedick.

Leonato O my lord, wisdom and blood combating in so tender a body, we have ten proofs to one that blood hath the victory. I am sorry for her, as I have just cause, being her uncle and her guardian.

Don Pedro I would she had bestowed this dotage on me. I would have doffed all other respects and made her half myself. I pray you tell Benedick of it and hear what he will say.

Leonato Were it good, think you?

Claudio Hero thinks surely she will die. For she says she will die if he love her not, and she will die ere she make her love known, and she will die if he woo her, rather than she will bate one breath of her accustomed crossness.

Don Pedro She doth well. If she should make tender of her love, 'tis very possible he'll scorn it, for the man (as you know all), hath a contemptible spirit.

Claudio He is a very proper man.

Don Pedro He hath indeed a good outward happiness.

Claudio Before God, and in my mind, very wise.

Don Pedro He doth indeed show some sparks that are like wit.

Claudio And I take him to be valiant.

Don Pedro As Hector, I assure you. And in the managing of quarrels you may say he is wise, for either he avoids them with great discretion, or undertakes them with a most Christian-like fear.

Leonato If he do fear God, 'a must necessarily keep peace. If he break the peace, he ought to enter into a quarrel with fear and trembling.

Don Pedro And so will he do, for the man doth fear God, howsoever it seems not in him by some large jests he will make. Well, I am sorry for your niece. Shall we go seek Benedick and tell him of her love?

Claudio Never tell him, my lord, let her wear it out with good counsel.

Leonato Nay that's impossible, she may wear her heart out first.

Don Pedro Well, we will hear further of it by your daughter. Let it cool the while. I love Benedick well, and I could wish he would modestly examine himself to see how much he is unworthy so good a lady.

Leonato My lord, will you walk? Dinner is ready.

Claudio *[Aside.]* If he do not dote on her upon this, I will never trust my expectation.

---

152 **blood:** passion

153 **we have ten proofs to one:** it's a good bet that

156 **bestowed this dotage on:** fallen this deeply in love with

157 **doffed all other respects:** cast aside all other considerations

157 **half myself:** my wife

163 **bate one breath of her accustomed crossness:** change her usual manner

164 **make tender of:** show

166 **hath a contemptible spirit:** he's scornful about everything

167 **proper:** good-looking

168 **good outward happiness:** good enough looks

170 **wit:** intelligence

172 **Hector:** a very brave Trojan warrior

173 **quarrels:** used here to mean duels

180 **howsoever it seems not in him:** though it doesn't seem so

183–4 **wear it out with good counsel:** take good advice and get over it eventually

191 **upon this:** after this

192 **my expectation:** my judgement about how things will turn out

FROM THE REHEARSAL ROOM...

MONOLOGUE AS DUOLOGUE

- In pairs, read Benedick's monologue as a duologue (lines 199–220).
- Each time you get to a full stop, question mark or exclamation mark, change reader until the next punctuation mark. Continue like this until you reach the end of line 220.

1 What is Benedick's view of marriage and women now?

2 Has Benedick changed his mind? You have answered this question before (page 42, question 4).

3 What has changed his mind?

***A* Beatrice calls Benedick to dinner, 2011.**

***B* Benedick, as Beatrice calls him to dinner, 2008.**

1 At which point do you think Photo A was taken? Give a line number, and quote from the text to support your answer.

2 At which point do you think Photo B was taken? Give a line number, and quote from the text to support your answer.

A Eve Best, Charles Edwards; ***B*** Bill Buckhurst

FROM THE REHEARSAL ROOM...

LOVE ON THE LINE

This is a repeat of the activity on pages 10 and 34. Look back to remind yourself of the instructions.

- Working in small groups, one person reads Benedick's soliloquy (lines 199–220). The rest of the group are 'listeners'.
- As the reader reads through the soliloquy, the 'listeners' should repeat, as a whisper, anything positive he says about Beatrice.

1 Where is Benedick on the line? Quote from the text to support your answer.

- Stand in the place on the line, and compare your answer with other groups. Use your quotes to support your view.

2 Record your answer, and the one that the majority of the class agree on.

Don Pedro *[Aside.]* Let there be the same net spread for her, and that must your daughter and her gentlewomen carry. The sport will be when they hold one an opinion of another's dotage, and no such matter. That's the scene that I would see, which will be merely a dumb-show. Let us send her to call him in to dinner.

Exit Don Pedro, Leonato, and Claudio.

Benedick *[He steps out.]* This can be no trick. The conference was sadly borne, they have the truth of this from Hero, they seem to pity the lady. It seems her affections have their full bent. Love me? Why, it must be requited. I hear how I am censured. They say I will bear myself proudly if I perceive the love come from her. They say too, that she will rather die than give any sign of affection. I did never think to marry. I must not seem proud. Happy are they that hear their detractions and can put them to mending. They say the lady is fair, 'tis a truth, I can bear them witness. And virtuous, 'tis so, I cannot reprove it. And wise, but for loving me. By my troth, it is no addition to her wit, nor no great argument of her folly, for I will be horribly in love with her. I may chance have some odd quirks and remnants of wit broken on me, because I have railed so long against marriage. But doth not the appetite alter? A man loves the meat in his youth that he cannot endure in his age. Shall quips and sentences and these paper bullets of the brain awe a man from the career of his humour? No, the world must be peopled. When I said I would die a bachelor, I did not think I should live till I were married. Here comes Beatrice. By this day, she's a fair lady. I do spy some marks of love in her.

Enter Beatrice.

Beatrice Against my will I am sent to bid you come in to dinner.

Benedick Fair Beatrice, I thank you for your pains.

Beatrice I took no more pains for those thanks than you take pains to thank me. If it had been painful, I would not have come.

Benedick You take pleasure then, in the message?

Beatrice Yea, just so much as you may take upon a knife's point, and choke a daw withal. You have no stomach signor? Fare you well. *Exit Beatrice.*

Benedick Ha! "Against my will I am sent to bid you come in to dinner." There's a double meaning in that. "I took no more pains for those thanks than you took pains to thank me." That's as much as to say, "Any pains that I take for you is as easy as thanks." If I do not take pity of her I am a villain. If I do not love her, I am a Jew. I will go get her picture.

Exit.

194 **carry:** carry out
195–6 **when they hold one … no such matter:** when each thinks the other is deeply in love, when neither of them are
197 **dumb-show:** mime (because both will be speechless)
200 **sadly borne:** in all seriousness
201–2 **have their full bent:** are stretched to the limit
202 **requited:** returned in equal measure
203 **censured:** criticised
207 **their detractions:** criticism of themselves
210 **reprove:** contradict
212–4 **I may chance … broken on me:** maybe I will be made fun of
217–8 **Shall quips and … humour?** should a man be put off doing what he wants by a few jokes?
230 **daw:** jackdaw
230 **withal:** with
230 **You have no stomach signor?:** Aren't you hungry, sir?
237 **I am a Jew:** I'm not a Christian (at the time, Christians were seen as kind, Jews as merciless)

Director's Note, 2.3

- ✔ Benedick wonders how Claudio can have changed so much since falling in love.
- ✔ Don Pedro, Leonato and Claudio enter and pretend not to see Benedick – who hides from them.
- ✔ Making sure Benedick can hear them, the talk about Beatrice's love for Benedick.
- ✔ They leave. Benedick, who is completely taken in, decides to return her love.
- ✔ When Beatrice comes to call him for dinner, he thinks he sees she loves him from the way she behaves.
- ✔ How many mistakes does Benedick make?

STUDY NOTES, 2.3

TIP

A good response

A good response may include more than one way of interpreting a scene. The key word is 'or'. For example, in this scene, Benedick's change of mind may make an audience feel that he is a foolish, fickle character. Or it could make an audience feel that he is behaving as many people do when they find it flattering to be told that someone is in love with them.

USING THE VIDEO

Exploring interpretation and performance

If you have looked at the video extracts in the online version try this question.

Usually the gulling scene is played with Benedick mainly concealed behind a garden hedge. In the 2008 production it is played on the open stage, with Benedick fully visible. How does the performance in the clip bring humour out of the way it is played? Do you think it works as well as if it was played with Benedick concealed, as in the 2004 clip?

1 Character and plot development

Shakespeare follows up the initial impressions created about the characters by showing the way they react to others and reveal things about themselves through soliloquies.

1 Shakespeare uses Benedick's soliloquy (lines 8–35) to convey the change in Claudio since falling in love. How does the soliloquy convey Benedick's attitudes to Claudio and to Love? Find the key words and phrases.

2 In what ways do Don Pedro, Claudio and Leonato play on Benedick's feelings in order to make him believe that Beatrice is in love with him (lines 117–66)? Look at what they say and how they say it.

3 Benedick's second soliloquy (lines 199–222) shows that Don Pedro's plan has worked. How does Shakespeare make his change of mind amusing, and how does the change of mind give the audience something to expect? Pick out words and phrases as examples.

4 What makes the audience look forward to further comic trickery in scenes that will follow? Can you find any evidence?

2 Characterisation and voice: dramatic language

Soliloquies and asides are useful devices to reveal what characters want to keep secret and what they say when they think no-one can hear them.

5 How does Shakespeare make Benedick's statements in his first soliloquy seem confident and unchangeable? Look at what he says and how he says it (lines 8–35).

6 What makes Benedick's second soliloquy (lines 199–222) seem like someone trying to make a complete change of mind seem reasonable and practical? Which lines suggest this?

7 This gulling scene makes much use of asides mixed with louder statements intended for Benedick to hear. How do these asides show the plotters' enjoyment of their game and Benedick's increasing belief that what they say is true? Choose words and phrases to support your points.

3 Themes and ideas

Some themes and ideas are simple and amusing. Others are more complex and may be serious. Shakespeare mingles the amusing and the serious in various ways in this play and in others.

8 Balthasar's song (lines 60–75) provides some theatrical variety but also has something to say about men and love. What makes the song connect with comic and serious aspects of the theme of deceit in the play? Which words might suggest this?

9 The theme of love is also developed here. When Beatrice comes out to call him in for dinner, she makes it clear (she thinks) that she does not want to speak to him (line 228). How does Shakespeare use the situation to show how much Benedick has changed, and interprets words and actions as a man influenced by love? Look at what he says and how he says it.

STUDY NOTES, 2.3

4 Performance

Trying different ways of playing parts of scenes is the best way of understanding how Shakespeare wanted to entertain his audience or make them feel suspense or surprise. You and your classmates can be the actors checking out how Shakespeare's script can best be performed.

10 If you were directing this gulling scene, would you have Benedick concealed from Don Pedro, Leonato and Claudio but continuously visible to the audience, or would you have him concealed and occasionally visible? Give reasons for your answer.

11 How would you advise the actor playing Balthasar? Would you advise him to sing and play badly, in line with his comments about being an 'ill singer', making it a comic performance, or would you advise him to sing and play perfectly, making the song an important part of the play's themes? Explain your preference by referring to the text (lines 36–82).

12 What would you advise Benedick to be doing during Balthasar's song to match his comment on the singing in lines 79–82? Give reasons for your answer.

13 How should the actor playing Benedick use voice and movement to convey his changed attitude during his brief talk with Beatrice and after? Think carefully about what he says (lines 223–38).

5 Contexts and responses

Although Shakespeare wrote for the audience he knew four hundred years ago, audiences today may respond in the same way – or they may have a different response. It's always worth asking how different kinds of audiences may react to a character, an event or a situation.

14 What would you suggest are modern equivalents of Benedick's examples of 'manly' interests over 'softer' interests, in his soliloquy on the change in Claudio (lines 8–35)?

15 How may a filmed version (rather than a stage version) of the scene bring out the humour of the gulling and the use of speech which is meant to be heard by Benedick and speech which is not meant to be heard by him?

6 Reflecting on the scene

16 How does Shakespeare make 'changing one's opinion' dramatically interesting in this scene?

17 Do you think Shakespeare has presented Benedick as a character we laugh at or as one we laugh with?

18 How has your appreciation of this scene been developed by a stage, screen or classroom performance?

TIP

Writing about drama

An audience watching a play must be gripped by what happens on stage, without reading the script.

Writing about a drama text needs to show how the plot is constructed to keep an audience interested, with shifts of scene and changes of character on stage, and lines which an actor can not only speak but perform with visible and audible emphasis.

TIP

Writing about drama

Show that you understand why Shakespeare uses dramatic devices; e.g., 'In the first soliloquy Shakespeare makes Benedick seem totally confident that he will never fall in love when he says "I will live a bachelor" and then change this in the second soliloquy to "When I said I would die a bachelor, I did not think I should live till I were married". The soliloquies show how he has changed his mind but doesn't want to admit that he has.'

TIP

Reflecting on the scene

Make sure you consider Shakespeare's skill in characterisation – making characters believable – and seeming real in performance on stage, representing important themes and ideas.

This will help you treat them as imaginary characters created by Shakespeare, rather than real people.

Beatrice in hiding, 2004.

1 Compare this with the photos of the gulling of Benedick (pages 44–48). What are the similarities?

2 We talk of Shakespeare giving stage directions in his text. What 'stage directions' in the text has the director followed in this case?

Yolanda Vazquez

SHAKESPEARE'S WORLD

Gentlewomen

In Shakespeare's day gentlewomen, like Margaret and Ursula who are Hero's gentlewomen, were not ordinary servants. They were from a higher social class than the ordinary servants – perhaps even from a family of the same class as their mistress – but one that had fallen on hard times. They would not clean or cook; and much of the time they spent with their mistress, almost like a friend. They were not quite a friend either, but somewhere between friend and an ordinary servant. Hero tells them what to do, but she also shares her secrets with them, as she does in this scene, involving them in the gulling of Benedick.

Actor's view

Yolanda Vazquez
Beatrice, 2004

Mariah [Gale, playing Hero] and I worked out these bits of business while I was hiding in the arbour. I'd look out of the arbour at certain times, and Mariah would try not to look at me. So we were playing this game of hide and seek, I'm hiding from them, and they're sort of hiding from me because, while they know I'm there, they have to make me think they don't know. One day, as we were doing a run, Mariah got it wrong. She kept on moving away from the arbour. I chose to run out (because otherwise I couldn't hear them) and then run back to the arbour. When we had finished the three of us thought we'd got it wrong, but the rest of the group were on the floor with laughter. We said we didn't know what was going on, but the rest of team were saying 'No, no, you must keep it. It's very funny.' So that's how that came about; complete accident.

ACT 3 SCENE 1

There is a bower on stage. Enter Hero, and two gentlewomen, Margaret, and Ursula.

Hero
Good Margaret, run thee to the parlour,
There shalt thou find my cousin Beatrice
Proposing with the Prince and Claudio.
Whisper her ear, and tell her I and Ursula
Walk in the orchard, and our whole discourse
Is all of her. Say that thou overheard'st us,
And bid her steal into the pleachèd bower
Where honeysuckles ripened by the sun,
Forbid the sun to enter, like favourites
Made proud by princes, that advance their pride
Against that power that bred it. There will she hide her
To listen our purpose. This is thy office,
Bear thee well in it, and leave us alone.

Margaret
I'll make her come, I warrant you, presently.
[Exit Margaret.]

Hero
Now Ursula, when Beatrice doth come,
As we do trace this alley up and down,
Our talk must only be of Benedick.
When I do name him, let it be thy part
To praise him more than ever man did merit.
My talk to thee must be how Benedick
Is sick in love with Beatrice. Of this matter
Is little Cupid's crafty arrow made,
That only wounds by hearsay. *[Beatrice enters and hides.]*
[To Ursula.] Now begin,
For look where Beatrice like a lapwing runs
Close by the ground, to hear our conference.

Ursula
[To Hero.] The pleasant'st angling is to see the fish
Cut with her golden oars the silver stream,
And greedily devour the treacherous bait.
So angle we for Beatrice, who even now
Is couchèd in the woodbine coverture.
Fear you not my part of the dialogue.

Hero
[To Ursula.] Then go we near her, that her ear lose nothing
[Aloud.] Of the false sweet bait that we lay for it.
[They walk towards the bower.]
No truly Ursula, she is too disdainful.
I know her spirits are as coy and wild
As haggards of the rock.

Ursula
But are you sure
That Benedick loves Beatrice so entirely?

Hero
So says the Prince and my new-trothèd lord.

Ursula
And did they bid you tell her of it, madam?

Hero
They did entreat me to acquaint her of it.

---

3 **Proposing:** talking
5 **discourse:** conversation
7 **pleachèd bower:** a path in a garden shaded by intertwined tress and creepers, in this case honeysuckle
9 **favourites:** people who princes give special attention to
10–1 **that advance their pride ... bred it:** who come to see themselves as better than their prince and turn on him
12 **purpose:** conversation
12 **office:** job
13 **Bear thee well in it:** do it well
14 **I warrant you:** I promise
16 **trace this alley up and down:** walk along this path
21 **Of this matter:** from things like this
23 **only wounds by hearsay:** wounds with nothing more than hearsay
24 **lapwing:** a bird that sometimes runs along the ground
26 **angling:** fishing
27 **oars:** fins
30 **couchèd in the woodbine coverture:** hiding behind the honeysuckle
31 **Fear you not my part of the dialogue:** don't worry, I know what to say
34 **disdainful:** scornful
35 **coy:** evasive
35 **wild:** uncontrollable
36 **haggards of the rock:** untamed female hawks living in wild places
38 **new-trothèd:** recently engaged to be married

A

Beatrice (hiding), Hero and Ursula: *A* (2011), *B* (2004), *C* (without Ursula, 2008).

1 Explain how each of the three productions solved the problem of staging this scene.
2 What advantages and disadvantages might there be with each solution?
3 How would you stage this scene? Explain your answer.

A Eve Best, Ony Uhiara, Helen Weir; ***B*** Mariah Gale, Yolanda Vazquez, Lucy Campbell; ***C*** Kirsty Besterman, Natasha Magigi

B

C

But I persuaded them, if they loved Benedick,
To wish him wrestle with affection,
And never to let Beatrice know of it.

Ursula Why did you so? Doth not the gentleman
Deserve as full, as fortunate a bed
As ever Beatrice shall couch upon?

Hero O God of Love! I know he doth deserve
As much as may be yielded to a man,
But Nature never framed a woman's heart
Of prouder stuff than that of Beatrice.
Disdain and scorn ride sparkling in her eyes,
Mis-prizing what they look on, and her wit
Values itself so highly that to her
All matter else seems weak. She cannot love,
Nor take no shape nor project of affection,
She is so self-endeared.

Ursula Sure I think so,
And therefore certainly it were not good
She knew his love, lest she'll make sport at it.

Hero Why, you speak truth. I never yet saw man
(How wise, how noble, young, how rarely featured),
But she would spell him backward. If fair-faced,
She would swear the gentleman should be her sister.
If black, why Nature, drawing of an antic,
Made a foul blot. If tall, a lance ill-headed.
If low, an agate very vilely cut.
If speaking, why, a vane blown with all winds.
If silent, why, a block movèd with none.
So turns she every man the wrong side out,
And never gives to truth and virtue that
Which simpleness and merit purchaseth.

- Knows Beatrice very ~~good~~ well

Ursula Sure, sure, such carping is not commendable.

Hero No, not to be so odd and from all fashions
As Beatrice is, cannot be commendable.
But who dare tell her so? If I should speak,
She would mock me into air. O she would laugh me
Out of myself, press me to death with wit.
Therefore let Benedick, like covered fire,
Consume away in sighs, waste inwardly.
It were a better death than die with mocks,
Which is as bad as die with tickling.

- wouldn't dare to start a ~~wit~~ merry war with her, is inferior to her, not quick at repartee

Ursula Yet tell her of it, hear what she will say.

Hero No, rather I will go to Benedick
And counsel him to fight against his passion.
And truly I'll devise some honest slanders
To stain my cousin with. One doth not know
How much an ill word may empoison liking.

Ursula O do not do your cousin such a wrong!
She cannot be so much without true judgment,

42 **wish him wrestle with affection:** advise him to fight this love
45–6 **as full, as fortunate a bed … couch upon:** a wife as good as Beatrice
52 **Mis-prizing:** undervaluing
53–4 **Values itself so highly that to her … seems weak:** is more important to her than anything else
55 **Nor take no shape nor project of affection:** or understand the idea of loving or being loved
56 **self-endeared:** in love with herself
60 **How:** no matter how
61 **spell him backward:** say he was the opposite
63 **black:** dark-complexioned
63 **drawing of an antic:** creating an ugly, misshapen creature
64 **lance ill-headed:** spear with the iron head badly made
65 **low:** short
65 **agate very vilely cut:** agates (semi-precious stones) were often decorated with tiny carvings and set in rings
66 **speaking:** talks a lot
70 **simpleness:** sincerity, plain speaking
70 **purchaseth:** deserves
71 **carping:** fault-finding
71 **commendable:** something to be praised
72 **from all fashions:** out of step
76 **press me to death with wit:** heap witty remarks on me until I couldn't breathe (pressing to death was a punishment at the time)
77 **covered fire:** a fire packed with fuel to burn slowly overnight
78 **Consume away in sighs, waste inwardly:** die slowly of undeclared love
79 **It were:** it would be
82 **rather:** instead
84 **honest slanders:** harmless lies

Working Cut – text for experiment

Ursula But are you sure
That Benedick loves Beatrice so entirely?
Hero So says the Prince and my new-trothèd lord.
Ursula And did they bid you tell her of it, madam?
Hero They did entreat me to acquaint her of it.
But I persuaded them, if they loved Benedick,
To wish him wrestle with affection,
And never to let Beatrice know of it.
Ursula Why did you so? Doth not the gentleman
Deserve as full, as fortunate a bed
As ever Beatrice shall couch upon?
Hero O God of Love! I know he doth deserve
As much as may be yielded to a man,
But Nature never framed a woman's heart
Of prouder stuff than that of Beatrice.
Disdain and scorn ride sparkling in her eyes,
She cannot love. She is so self-endeared.
Ursula And therefore certainly it were not good
She knew his love, lest she'll make sport at it.
Hero Why, you speak truth. I never yet saw man
How wise, how noble, young, how rarely featured),
But she would spell him backward.
Ursula Sure, sure, such carping is not commendable
Hero But who dare tell her so?
Therefore let Benedick, like covered fire,
Consume away in sighs, waste inwardly.
Ursula Yet tell her of it, hear what she will say.
Hero No, rather I will go to Benedick
And counsel him to fight against his passion.
Ursula O do not do your cousin such a wrong!
She cannot be so much without true judgment,
Having so swift and excellent a wit
As she is prized to have, as to refuse
So rare a gentleman as Signor Benedick.
Hero He is the only man of Italy,
Always excepted my dear Claudio.
Ursula I pray you be not angry with me, madam
Speaking my fancy. Signior Benedick,
Goes foremost in report through Italy.

Director's Note, 3.1

- ✔ Beatrice is tricked into thinking she is overhearing a private conversation between Hero and Ursula.
- ✔ She is shocked to hear them talk about how much Benedick loves her, and that it is a good thing she doesn't know, because she is so proud and scornful.
- ✔ Hero and Ursula leave, and Beatrice decides she will love Benedick.
- ✔ How important are the mistakes in this scene?

FROM THE REHEARSAL ROOM...

TACTICS

Ursula and Hero are tricking Beatrice into believing that Benedick loves her. While Beatrice is hiding, the women use different tactics to convince her.

- In pairs, label yourselves **A** and **B**.
- Decide on a gesture for these four tactics: Hook, Lure, Concern and Shock. Make sure that each gesture is a strong action and represents the tactic. *For example, Hook is about bringing somebody to agree with you. Use a gesture where your hand is bent up like a hook, bringing them towards you.*
- Now read the *Working Cut*. As you say each line decide if it uses one of these tactics, and if it does, use the gesture.
- Discuss and agree which tactics Ursula and Hero use at different points in the text. Add another tactic of your own if you think you need it.
- Read Beatrice's soliloquy at the end of the scene.

1. Give an example of how Hero and Ursula use each tactic.
2. How do the different tactics affect Beatrice?
3. Which tactic do you think was the most effective? Support your answer with evidence from the text.

FROM THE REHEARSAL ROOM...

LOVE ON THE LINE

This is a repeat of the activity on pages 10, 34 and 50. Look back at the instructions.

- Working in small groups, one person reads Beatrice's soliloquy (lines 108–117). The rest are 'listeners'.
- As the reader reads through the soliloquy, the 'listeners' should repeat, as a whisper, anything positive she says about Benedick.

1. Where is Beatrice on the line? Quote from the text to support your answer.

- Compare your answer with other groups.

2. Record your answer, and the one that the majority of the class agree on.

	Having so swift and excellent a wit As she is prized to have, as to refuse So rare a gentleman as Signor Benedick.
Hero	He is the only man of Italy, Always excepted my dear Claudio. *in love—*
Ursula	I pray you be not angry with me, madam, Speaking my fancy. Signior Benedick, For shape, for bearing, argument and valour, Goes foremost in report through Italy.
Hero	Indeed, he hath an excellent good name.
Ursula	His excellence did earn it ere he had it. When are you married, madam?
Hero	Why, every day, tomorrow. Come, go in, I'll show thee some attires, and have thy counsel Which is the best to furnish me tomorrow.
Ursula	*[To Hero.]* She's limed, I warrant you, We have caught her, madam.
Hero	*[To Ursula.]* If it prove so, then loving goes by haps, Some Cupid kills with arrows, some with traps.
	Exit Hero and Ursula.
Beatrice	*[Coming out of the bower.]* What fire is in mine ears? Can this be true? Stand I condemned for pride and scorn so much? Contempt, farewell, and maiden pride, adieu. No glory lives behind the back of such. And Benedick, love on, I will requite thee, Taming my wild heart to thy loving hand. If thou dost love, my kindness shall incite thee To bind our loves up in a holy band. For others say thou dost deserve, and I Believe it better than reportingly. *Exit.*

ACT 3 SCENE 2

Enter Don Pedro, Claudio, Benedick, and Leonato.

Don Pedro	I do but stay till your marriage be consummate, and then go I toward Aragon.
Claudio	I'll bring you thither my lord, if you'll vouchsafe me.
Don Pedro	Nay, that would be as great a soil in the new gloss of your marriage as to show a child his new coat and forbid him to wear it. I will only be bold with Benedick for his company, for, from the crown of his head to the sole of his foot, he is all mirth. He hath twice or thrice cut Cupid's bowstring, and the little hangman dare not shoot at him. He hath a heart as sound as a bell, and his tongue is the clapper, for what his heart thinks, his tongue speaks.

Glossary:
- 90 **prized to have:** famous for
- 92 **the only:** the best
- 95 **my fancy:** what I think
- 97 **Goes foremost in report:** is most widely praised
- 99 **ere:** before
- 101 **every day, tomorrow:** tomorrow and every day after
- 102 **attires:** clothes or headdresses
- 103 **to furnish me:** for me to wear
- 104 **She's limed:** trapped (bird lime was a sap used for catching small birds)
- 106 **haps:** chance, accident
- 108 **What fire is in mine ears:** my ears are burning (from being talked of)
- 111 **No glory lives behind the back of such:** behaviour like that is shameful
- 114 **incite:** spur you on
- 115 **holy band:** wedding ring
- 117 **better than reportingly:** she feels it is true, as well as overhearing it

- 3 **bring you thither:** escort you there
- 3 **vouchsafe:** allow
- 6 **only be bold with:** just take
- 9 **the little hangman:** i.e. Cupid
- 11 **clapper:** the piece inside the bell that strikes it

A Leonato, Claudio, Benedick, Don Pedro, 2004.

B Benedick, 2008.

Compare Photo A with earlier photos of Benedick in the 2004 production (pages 10 and 46).
Compare Photo B with earlier photos of Benedick from the 2008 production (pages 46 and 50).

Both these productions picked up a possible stage direction in the text. What is it? Quote the passage from the text to support your answer.

A Penelope Beaumont, Ann Ogbomo, Josie Lawrence, Belinda Davison ***B*** Bill Buckhurst

SHAKESPEARE'S WORLD

Stage directions in the text

When first printed, Shakespeare's plays did not have many stage directions. What Shakespeare often does is make it clear to the actor what to do, by what he makes somebody in the scene say. We call these things *stage directions in the text*. Most of them are obvious; for example, in *Macbeth* Banquo says to his son:

Hold, take my sword.

Clearly, at this point, the actor playing Banquo passes over his sword.

Benedick	Gallants, I am not as I have been.	
Leonato	So say I, methinks you are sadder. *changed*	14 **sadder:** more serious, or melancholy (lovers were thought to be melancholy)
Claudio	I hope he be in love.	15 *makes fun of him*
Don Pedro	Hang him, truant! There's no true drop of blood in him to be truly touched with love. If he be sad, he wants money.	17 **wants:** lacks
Benedick	I have the toothache.	
Don Pedro	Draw it.	19 **Draw it:** pull it out
Benedick	Hang it! 20	20 **Hang it!:** a curse (Don Pedro then puns on hanging and drawing, a punishment at the time)
Claudio	You must hang it first, and draw it afterwards.	
Don Pedro	What? Sigh for the toothache?	
Leonato	Where is but a humour or a worm.	23 **Where is but:** for nothing more than
Benedick	Well, everyone can master a grief but he that has it.	23 **a humour or a worm:** two things people at the time thought caused toothache
Claudio	Yet say I, he is in love. 25	24 **master:** overcome
Don Pedro	There is no appearance of fancy in him, unless it be a fancy that he hath to strange disguises, as to be a Dutchman today, a Frenchman tomorrow, or in the shape of two countries at once, as a German from the waist downward, all slops, and a Spaniard from the 30 hip upward, no doublet. Unless he have a fancy to this foolery, as it appears he hath, he is no fool for fancy, as you would have it appear he is.	24 **but:** except 26–7 **fancy … fancy:** love … fad (in fashion) followed by a discussion of fashion
Claudio	If he be not in love with some woman, there is no believing old signs. 'A brushes his hat o'mornings. What 35 should that bode?	35 **'A:** He 36 **bode:** foretell
Don Pedro	Hath any man seen him at the barber's?	
Claudio	No, but the barber's man hath been seen with him, and the old ornament of his cheek hath already stuffed tennis balls. 40	39 **the old ornament of his cheek:** his beard 39–40 **stuffed tennis balls:** they were stuffed with hair at the time
Leonato	Indeed he looks younger than he did, by the loss of a beard.	
Don Pedro	Nay, 'a rubs himself with civet. Can you smell him out by that?	43 **civet:** perfume
Claudio	That's as much as to say, the sweet youth's in love. 45	46 **note:** sign
Don Pedro	The greatest note of it is his melancholy.	47 **when was he wont to:** when did he ever
Claudio	And when was he wont to wash his face?	48 **paint himself:** wear make-up (which some men did at the time)
Don Pedro	Yea, or to paint himself? For the which I hear what they say of him.	48–9 **For the which I hear what they say of him:** which is causing a lot of talk
Claudio	Nay but his jesting spirit, which is now crept into a 50 lute-string and now governed by stops.	51 **lute-string:** a lute was a stringed musical instrument like a small guitar with a pear-shaped face and a rounded back. They were used to play love songs
Don Pedro	Indeed that tells a heavy tale for him. Conclude, conclude, he is in love.	51 **stops:** frets (used in lutes like they are in guitars)
Claudio	Nay, but I know who loves him.	

Claudio and Don Pedro, 2011.

1 Was this photo taken before or after Don John makes his accusation about Hero? Give reasons for your answer.

2 Why is Don Pedro looking at Claudio? Explain your answer.

Philip Cumbus, Ewan Stewart

Actor's view

Philip Cumbus
Claudio, 2011

He has an instinctive an impulse to fight, and an impulse to hit and to react physically to any situation. And that came out in the scene. People thought, at that particular juncture in the scene, that I might actually hit him, which I wanted, I wanted people to believe that this was a man who was capable of that. And then something else happens in that scene, Claudio goes to a different place in his brain, he doesn't do that and I wanted to show that shift from that choice not to hit Don John. And it happens because it taps into an insecurity in him that I think we explored earlier in the play; that there is a level of self doubt in Claudio that I found useful at this point. Because the moment it is suggested that she is unfaithful, he believes it, he thinks it's possible, and that's because I don't think he ever fully believes that she might love him. He hasn't spoken a single word to this girl, he doesn't know her at all and yet suddenly they're going to get married, suddenly they're betrothed to each other. And this situation comes along whereby he's told she has been unfaithful and I believe he is a man who would hear that about somebody that he didn't know and would possibly think that it might be true. Some people imagine that this is a relationship where they can discuss things, they go, 'Well why doesn't Claudio just go and talk to her about it? Why doesn't he check the facts out before he shames her?' And actually, that's not the situation they're in. He hasn't got that ability. He knows nothing about her and then he's led, after this scene, to go and see some physical evidence of it.

Actor's view

Matthew Pidgeon
Don John, 2011

There was a belief [at the time] that if you were a bastard there was something in your blood – there was something actively wrong with you – that meant you were sort of devious, and envious, and melancholic and all these things. You can either believe that or you can just believe that if he's a bastard he's been treated in a certain way all his life which is going to potentially make him envious, devious, melancholy. He is the dark cloud, isn't he, in this fun thing? You can't play him as funny-funny or as 'ho, ho, ho, I'm a baddie', twirling a moustache. You've just got to play his situation, his dilemmas. He feels justified in trying to bring these people down, he feels that he's been hard done by in life. And that is his nature. In fact, in the scenes where he talks about it, he doesn't try to hide it. He says, 'this is the way I am, a bastard, I can't be any other way.'

Without him you don't get that depth and that darkness. Other characters are tested by his actions and drama comes out of that. And actually he pushes on the Beatrice and Benedick relationship through his actions. So he is absolutely essential to the play – the other characters react, the drama occurs, because of this dark cloud, this weight, this heavy thing that is dragging the joy down a little bit.

Don Pedro That would I know too, I warrant, one that knows him not.

Claudio Yes, and his ill conditions, and in despite of all, dies for him.

Don Pedro She shall be buried with her face upwards.

Benedick Yet is this no charm for the toothache. *[To Leonato.]* Old signor, walk aside with me. I have studied eight or nine wise words to speak to you, which these hobby-horses must not hear. *[Exit Benedick and Leonato.]*

Don Pedro For my life, to break with him about Beatrice!

Claudio 'Tis even so. Hero and Margaret have by this played their parts with Beatrice, and then the two bears will not bite one another when they meet.

Enter Don John, 'the Bastard'.

Don John My lord and brother, God save you.

Don Pedro Good e'en, brother.

Don John If your leisure served, I would speak with you.

Don Pedro In private?

Don John If it please you, yet Count Claudio may hear, for what I would speak of concerns him.

Don Pedro What's the matter?

Don John *[To Claudio.]* Means your lordship to be married tomorrow?

Don Pedro You know he does.

Don John I know not that, when he knows what I know.

Claudio If there be any impediment, I pray you discover it.

Don John You may think I love you not. Let that appear hereafter, and aim better at me by that I now will manifest. For my brother (I think he holds you well, and in dearness of heart), hath holp to effect your ensuing marriage: surely suit ill spent and labour ill bestowed.

Don Pedro Why, what's the matter?

Don John I came hither to tell you, and circumstances shortened, (for she has been too long a-talking of), the lady is disloyal.

Claudio Who? Hero?

Don John Even she. Leonato's Hero, your Hero, every man's Hero.

Claudio Disloyal?

Don John The word is too good to paint out her wickedness. I could say she were worse. Think you of a worse title, and I will fit her to it. Wonder not till further warrant. Go but with me tonight, you shall see her chamber window entered, even the night before her wedding day. If you love her then, tomorrow wed her. But it would better fit your honour to change your mind.

56 **ill conditions:** bad qualities

57 **buried with her face upwards:** suggesting sex with Benedick

60 **hobby-horses:** jokers, fools

62 **break:** speak

68 **If your leisure served:** if you've got time

76 **I know not that:** It might not happen

77 **impediment:** reason not to marry

77 **discover:** reveal

78–9 **Let that appear … I now will manifest:** you'll change your mind when you hear what I have to say

80 **holds you well:** thinks well of you

81 **hath holp to effect:** has helped to arrange

82 **suit:** courtship

83 **what's the matter?:** what are you talking about?

84 **circumstances shortened:** in brief

85 **disloyal:** unfaithful

90 **paint out:** give a full picture of

92 **Wonder not till further warrant:** don't question it; I have proof

96 **better fit your honour:** be better for your reputation

Claudio May this be so?

Don Pedro I will not think it.

Don John If you dare not trust that you see, confess not that you know. If you will follow me, I will show you enough, and when you have seen more and heard more, proceed accordingly.

Claudio If I see anything tonight why I should not marry her, tomorrow in the congregation where I should wed, there will I shame her.

Don Pedro And as I wooed for thee to obtain her, I will join with thee to disgrace her.

Don John I will disparage her no farther till you are my witnesses. Bear it coldly but till midnight, and let the issue show itself.

Don Pedro O day untowardly turned!

Claudio O mischief strangely thwarting!

Don John O plague right well prevented! So will you say when you have seen the sequel.

They all exit.

99–100 **If you dare not ... you know:** you will only think she is innocent if you don't trust the evidence of your own eyes
108 **disparage her no farther:** say nothing more against her
109 **Bear it coldly:** act calmly
111 **untowardly turned:** gone badly wrong
112 **mischief strangely thwarting:** what an evil obstruction to my plans
114 **the sequel:** what follows

Director's Note, 3.2

- ✔ Don Pedro and Claudio tease Benedick about the change in his behaviour.
- ✔ Don John sets his trap for Claudio, telling him he can prove Hero is unfaithful, by showing her letting a man into her bedroom through the window that night.
- ✔ Don Pedro and Claudio agree to go with Don John and see what happens.

ACT 3 SCENE 3

Enter Dogberry, the Constable, Verges, his colleague, and the men of the Watch, including George Seacole and Hugh Oatcake.

Dogberry Are you good men and true?

Verges Yea, or else it were pity but they should suffer salvation, body and soul.

Dogberry Nay, that were a punishment too good for them, if they should have any allegiance in them, being chosen for the Prince's Watch.

Verges Well, give them their charge, neighbour Dogberry.

Dogberry First, who think you the most desertless man to be constable?

First Watchman Hugh Oatcake, sir, or George Seacole, for they can write and read.

Dogberry Come hither neighbour Seacole. God hath blessed you with a good name. To be a well-favoured man is the gift of fortune, but to write and read comes by nature.

Seacole Both which, Master Constable —

Dogberry You have. I knew it would be your answer. Well, for your favour sir, why give God thanks and make no boast of it, and for your writing and reading, let that appear when there is no need of such vanity. You are thought here to be the most senseless and fit man for

1 **true:** honest
3 **salvation:** he means 'damnation' (Verges and Dogberry often say the wrong word – sometimes one with an opposite meaning)
5 **allegiance:** loyalty: here he means 'disloyalty'
7 **charge:** instructions
8 **desertless:** unworthy: here he means 'worthy'
9 **constable:** the man in charge of this watch for Dogberry
13 **well-favoured:** handsome
14 **comes by nature:** you are born knowing; he means 'you are taught'
20 **senseless:** he means 'sensible'

SHAKESPEARE'S WORLD

The Watch and the Constable

In Shakespeare's time, there was no official police force. The Watch was made up by ordinary men, with no real training. It was more like our Neighbourhood Watch than our police force. All citizens had a duty to serve on the Watch for a certain number of days. In this way, everyone shared the job of looking after their community. It was unpaid, so men were often unenthusiastic, especially if there might be any danger. Many men did not want to take part at all. Richer citizens sometimes paid people to take their place on duty. A Constable was in charge of the watchmen to make sure they did their job correctly. However, constables were not trained professionals either, and the quality of constables varied widely. Some were educated and took their job seriously. Others were not. Part of the humour for people in the original audience was that they knew the Watch was often not much good. Dogberry, Verges and the Watch were just exaggerations.

Dogberry (in front, red jacket), Verges (on the right), and the Watch, 2011.

Which of the Watch is George Seacole? Give reasons for your answer.

Paul Hunter, Adrian Hood

the constable of the Watch. Therefore bear you the lantern. This is your charge: you shall comprehend all vagrom men, you are to bid any man stand, in the Prince's name.

Seacole How if 'a will not stand?

Dogberry Why then take no note of him, but let him go and presently call the rest of the Watch together, and thank God you are rid of a knave.

Verges If he will not stand when he is bidden, he is none of the Prince's subjects.

Dogberry True, and they are to meddle with none but the Prince's subjects. You shall also make no noise in the streets, for, for the Watch to babble and to talk is most tolerable, and not to be endured.

Seacole We will rather sleep than talk, we know what belongs to a watch.

Dogberry Why, you speak like an ancient and most quiet watchman, for I cannot see how sleeping should offend. Only have a care that your bills be not stolen. Well, you are to call at all the alehouses, and bid those that are drunk get them to bed.

Seacole How if they will not?

Dogberry Why then, let them alone till they are sober. If they make you not then the better answer, you may say they are not the men you took them for.

22 **comprehend:** he means 'apprehend': arrest
23 **vagrom:** he means 'vagrant'
23 **stand:** 'halt'
25 **'a:** he
27 **presently:** immediately
29 **bidden:** commanded
29 **none of:** not one of
33 **tolerable:** he means 'intolerable': unbearable
35–6 **belongs to:** is proper behaviour for
37 **ancient:** experienced
39 **bills:** weapons

Seacole Well, sir.

Dogberry If you meet a thief, you may suspect him, by virtue of your office, to be no true man. And for such kind of men, the less you meddle or make with them, why, the more is for your honesty.

Seacole If we know him to be a thief, shall we not lay hands on him?

Dogberry Truly, by your office you may, but I think they that touch pitch will be defiled. The most peaceable way for you, if you do take a thief, is to let him show himself what he is, and steal out of your company.

Verges You have been always called a merciful man, partner.

Dogberry Truly, I would not hang a dog by my will, much more a man who hath any honesty in him.

Verges If you hear a child cry in the night, you must call to the nurse and bid her still it.

Seacole How if the nurse be asleep and will not hear us?

Dogberry Why then, depart in peace and let the child wake her with crying, for the ewe that will not hear her lamb when it baas will never answer a calf when he bleats.

Verges 'Tis very true.

Dogberry This is the end of the charge: you, constable, are to present the Prince's own person. If you meet the Prince in the night, you may stay him.

Verges Nay by'r Lady, that I think 'a cannot.

Dogberry Five shillings to one on't with any man that knows the statues. He may stay him, marry not without the Prince be willing, for indeed the Watch ought to offend no man, and it is an offence to stay a man against his will.

Verges By'r Lady, I think it be so.

Dogberry Ha ha ha! Well, masters, good night. An there be any matter of weight chances, call up me. Keep your fellows' counsels and your own, and good night. Come, neighbour. *[They start to exit.]*

Seacole *[To the Watch.]* Well masters, we hear our charge. Let us go sit here upon the church bench till two, and then all to bed.

Dogberry One word more, honest neighbours. I pray you watch about Signor Leonato's door, for the wedding being there tomorrow, there is a great coil tonight. Adieu. Be vigitant, I beseech you.

Exit Dogberry and Verges.

Enter Borachio and Conrade.

Borachio What, Conrade?

49 **meddle or make:** have to do with

51 **lay hands on:** arrest

53–4 **they that touch pitch will be defiled:** a saying that means if you mix with bad people they will influence your behaviour

58 **more:** he means 'less'

61 **still:** quieten

67 **the charge:** your instructions

68 **present the Prince's own person:** represent the Prince

70 **by'r Lady:** by our Lady (the Virgin Mary), an oath to emphasise what is said

71–2 **Five shillings to one on't … knows the statutes:** I bet you five to one that anyone who knows the law will say so

72 **marry:** 'by the Virgin Mary' – an expression of surprise

72–3 **not without the Prince be willing:** as long as the Prince agrees

77 **any matter of weight:** anything important

77 **chances:** happens

77–8 **Keep your fellows' counsels and your own:** be discrete

85 **coil:** bustle, coming and going

86 **vigitant:** he means 'vigilant'

Seacole *[To the Watch.]* Peace, stir not.

Borachio Conrade I say!

Conrade Here man, I am at thy elbow.

Borachio Mass, and my elbow itched, I thought there would a scab follow.

Conrade I will owe thee an answer for that, and now forward with thy tale.

Borachio Stand thee close then under this penthouse, for it drizzles rain, and I will, like a true drunkard, utter all to thee.

Seacole *[To the Watch.]* Some treason, masters. Yet stand close.

Borachio Therefore know, I have earned of Don John a thousand ducats.

Conrade Is it possible that any villainy should be so dear?

Borachio Thou shouldst rather ask if it were possible any villainy should be so rich? For when rich villains have need of poor ones, poor ones may make what price they will.

Conrade I wonder at it.

Borachio That shows thou art unconfirmed. Thou knowest that the fashion of a doublet, or a hat, or a cloak, is nothing to a man.

Conrade Yes, it is apparel.

Borachio I mean the fashion.

Conrade Yes, the fashion is the fashion.

Borachio Tush, I may as well say the fool's the fool. But seest thou not what a deformed thief this fashion is?

First Watchman I know that Deformed. 'A has been a vile thief this seven year. 'A goes up and down like a gentle man. I remember his name.

Borachio Didst thou not hear somebody?

Conrade No, 'twas the vane on the house.

Borachio Seest thou not, I say, what a deformed thief this fashion is. How giddily 'a turns about all the hot bloods between fourteen and five-and-thirty, sometimes fashioning them like Pharaoh's soldiers in the reechy painting, sometime like god Bel's priests in the old church window, sometime like the shaven Hercules in the smirched worm-eaten tapestry, where his codpiece seems as massy as his club.

Conrade All this I see, and I see that the fashion wears out more apparel than the man. But art not thou thyself giddy with the fashion too, that thou hast shifted out of thy tale into telling me of the fashion?

91 **Mass:** by the Mass (an oath)
91 **and:** if
92 **scab:** double meaning: 1) dried blood from a cut; 2) a villain
95 **penthouse:** overhanging roof or upper floor of a building
96 **utter all to thee:** tell you everything
97 **Yet stand close:** stay hidden for now
100 **dear:** expensive
105 **unconfirmed:** inexperienced
106 **the fashion of a doublet:** the style of a jacket
106–7 **is nothing to a man:** tell us nothing about the wearer
108 **apparel:** just clothes
112 **what a deformed thief this fashion is:** how styles steal money (by making you buy new clothes before the old wear out)
113 **Deformed:** mistaking 'deformed' for a person
117 **vane:** weather-vane
119 **hot bloods:** vain, pushy young men
121 **fashioning them:** dressing them up
121 **reechy:** smoke-stained
122 **Bel:** Baal, a god worshipped in ancient times
124 **codpiece:** decorative pouch attached to the crotch of men's clothing
125 **massy:** huge

Borachio Not so, neither. But know that I have tonight wooed Margaret, the Lady Hero's gentlewoman, by the name of Hero. She leans me out at her mistress' chamber window, bids me a thousand times good night. — I tell this tale vilely. I should first tell thee how the Prince, Claudio and my master, planted and placed and possessed by my master Don John, saw afar off in the orchard this amiable encounter.

Conrade And thought they Margaret was Hero?

Boarchio Two of them did, the Prince and Claudio, but the devil my master knew she was Margaret. And partly by his oaths, which first possessed them, partly by the dark night, which did deceive them, but chiefly by my villainy, which did confirm any slander that Don John had made. Away went Claudio enraged, swore he would meet her as he was appointed next morning at the temple, and there, before the whole congregation, shame her with what he saw o'ernight, and send her home again without a husband.

First Watchman *[To Conrade and Borachio.]* We charge you in the Prince's name, stand!

Seacole Call up the right Master Constable. We have here recovered the most dangerous piece of lechery that ever was known in the commonwealth.

First Watchman And one Deformed is one of them. I know him, 'a wears a lock.

Conrade Masters, masters —

Seacole You'll be made. Bring Deformed forth, I warrant you.

Conrade Masters —

Seacole Never speak, we charge you, let us obey you to go with us.

Borachio *[To Conrade.]* We are like to prove a goodly commodity, being taken up of these men's bills.

Conrade *[To Borachio.]* A commodity in question I warrant you. — Come, we'll obey you.

The Watch leads off Borachio and Conrade.

135–6 **planted and placed and possessed:** manipulated
137 **amiable:** loving
141 **possessed them:** took over their minds
146 **before:** in front of
147 **o'ernight:** the previous night
152 **recovered:** he means 'discovered'
152 **lechery:** he means 'treachery'
154–5 **'a wears a lock:** he has one long lock of hair (a fashion at the time)
159 **obey you:** he means 'order you'
160 **goodly commodity:** fine purchases
161 **taken up of these men's bills:** double meaning: 1) arrested by men armed like this; 2) bought on credit ('bills' promise payment)
162 **in question:** double meaning: 1) in demand; 2) of disputed ownership

Director's Note, 3.3

- ✔ A comic scene. Dogberry and Verges tell the Watch their duties.
- ✔ The Watch overhear Borachio tell Conrade how the plot completely fooled Claudio and Don Pedro.
- ✔ The Watch arrest Conrade and Borachio.

ACT 3 SCENE 4

Enter Hero, Margaret, and Ursula.

Hero Good Ursula, wake my cousin Beatrice and desire her to rise.

Ursula I will lady.

Hero And bid her come hither.

Ursula Well. *Exit.*

Margaret Troth, I think your other rebato were better.

6 **Troth:** in truth
6 **rebato:** a collar or ruff with a wire frame

Hero No, pray thee good Meg, I'll wear this.

Margaret By my troth, 's not so good, and I warrant your cousin will say so.

Hero My cousin's a fool, and thou art another. I'll wear none but this.

Margaret I like the new tire within excellently, if the hair were a thought browner. And your gown's a most rare fashion i' faith. I saw the Duchess of Milan's gown that they praise so.

Hero O that exceeds, they say.

Margaret By my troth, 's but a nightgown in respect of yours: cloth-o'-gold and cuts, and laced with silver, set with pearls, down sleeves, side-sleeves, and skirts round underborne with a bluish tinsel. But for a fine, quaint, graceful, and excellent fashion, yours is worth ten on't.

Hero God give me joy to wear it, for my heart is exceeding heavy.

Margaret 'Twill be heavier soon by the weight of a man.

Hero Fie upon thee, art not ashamed?

Margaret Of what, lady? Of speaking honourably? Is not marriage honourable in a beggar? Is not your lord honourable without marriage? I think you would have me say, saving your reverence, "a husband." An bad thinking do not wrest true speaking, I'll offend nobody. Is there any harm in "the heavier for a husband"? None, I think, an it be the right husband and the right wife, otherwise 'tis light, and not heavy. Ask my Lady Beatrice else, here she comes.

Enter Beatrice.

Hero Good morrow coz.

Beatrice Good morrow sweet Hero.

Hero Why, how now? Do you speak in the sick tune?

Beatrice I am out of all other tune, methinks.

Margaret Clap's into "Light o' love," (that goes without a burden). Do you sing it, and I'll dance it.

Beatrice Ye "Light o' love" with your heels! Then if your husband have stables enough, you'll see he shall lack no barns.

Margaret O illegitimate construction! I scorn that with my heels.

Beatrice 'Tis almost five o'clock, cousin, 'tis time you were ready. By my troth, I am exceeding ill. Heigh-ho!

Margaret For a hawk, a horse, or a husband?

Beatrice For the letter that begins them all, H.

Margaret Well, an you be not turned Turk, there's no more sailing by the star.

12 **tire:** headdress with hair and ornaments on it
12 **within:** in her dressing room (not yet put on)
12–3 **a thought browner:** slightly browner (to match Hero's)
16 **exceeds:** is the best dress ever
17 **in respect of:** compared to
18 **cuts:** ornamental cuts to let the fabric underneath show through
18 **laced:** trimmed with
19 **down sleeves:** tight, long under-sleeves
19 **side-sleeves:** loose, partly open, over sleeves that show the ones underneath
19–20 **round underborne:** completely lined
20 **quaint:** elegant
21 **on't:** of it
25 **Fie upon thee:** don't be so disgusting
29 **saving your reverence:** excuse me (said ironically) because she's been accused of being rude
29–30 **An bad thinking do not wrest true speaking:** if your taking my remark the wrong way doesn't distort my meaning
33 **light:** double meaning: 1) not serious; 2) sexually promiscuous
37 **Do you speak in the sick tune?:** Aren't you well? You sound awful
39 **Clap's into:** clap the introduction to
39 **goes without a burden:** needs no male singer; needs no man (sexually)
41 **Ye "Light o' love" with your heels:** you're certainly 'light heeled': promiscuous
42 **barns:** implying 'bairns' – children
43 **illegitimate construction:** wrong interpretation, but also referring to the children mentioned in the previous line
45 **Heigh-ho!:** she sighs
47 **H:** at the time the letter 'h' and 'ache' were pronounced the same
48 **be not turned Turk:** have not changed your beliefs (Turks weren't Christian)
48–9 **there's no more sailing by the star:** nothing's certain anymore

Beatrice What means the fool, trow?

Margaret Nothing I, but God send every one their heart's desire.

Hero These gloves the Count sent me, they are an excellent perfume.

Beatrice I am stuffed, cousin, I cannot smell.

Margaret A maid, and stuffed! There's goodly catching of cold.

Beatrice O God help me, God help me! How long have you professed apprehension?

Margaret Ever since you left it. Doth not my wit become me rarely?

Beatrice It is not seen enough. You should wear it in your cap. By my troth I am sick.

Margaret Get you some of this distilled *carduus benedictus* and lay it on your heart, it is the only thing for a qualm.

Hero There thou prickest her with a thistle.

Beatrice *Benedictus?* Why *benedictus?* You have some moral in this *Benedictus?*

Margaret Moral? No, by my troth, I have no moral meaning, I meant, plain holy thistle. You may think perchance that I think you are in love. Nay, by'r lady, I am not such a fool to think what I list, nor I list not to think what I can, nor indeed I cannot think, if I would think my heart out of thinking, that you are in love, or that you will be in love, or that you can be in love. Yet Benedick was such another, and now is he become a man. He swore he would never marry, and yet now in despite of his heart, he eats his meat without grudging. And how you may be converted I know not, but methinks you look with your eyes as other women do.

Beatrice What pace is this that thy tongue keeps?

Margaret Not a false gallop.

Enter Ursula.

Ursula Madam, withdraw. The Prince, the Count, Signor Benedick, Don John, and all the gallants of the town are come to fetch you to church.

Hero Help to dress me good coz, good Meg, good Ursula.

They all exit.

50 **trow:** do you think
54 **stuffed:** bunged up with cold
55 **A maid, and stuffed:** refers to both sex and pregnancy
57 **professed apprehension:** thought you could be witty
58 **rarely:** excellently
61 ***carduus benedictus*:** a medicinal plant, like a thistle (but also refers to Benedick)
62 **a qualm:** sudden nausea
63 **There thou prickest her with a thistle:** Beatrice has reacted to Benedick's name
64 **You have some moral in:** you're making some kind of point with
67 **perchance:** perhaps
69 **list:** choose
73 **was such another:** was just like that, anti-love
75 **he eats his meat without grudging:** he loves without complaint
79 **Not a false gallop:** I'm not lying

Director's Note, 3.4

- ✔ Hero is getting ready for her wedding.
- ✔ When Beatrice arrives she says she has a cold, but they tease her about Benedick.

ACT 3 SCENE 5

Enter Leonato, Dogberry and Verges.

Leonato What would you with me, honest neighbour?

Dogberry Marry, sir, I would have some confidence with you, that decerns you nearly.

2 **confidence:** he means 'conference': private discussion
3 **decerns:** he means 'concerns'
3 **nearly:** here, it means personally

Leonato Brief I pray you, for you see it is a busy time with me.

Dogberry Marry, this it is, sir.

Verges Yes, in truth it is, sir.

Leonato What is it, my good friends?

Dogberry Goodman Verges, sir, speaks a little off the matter. An old man, sir, and his wits are not so blunt as, God help I would desire they were, but in faith, honest as the skin between his brows.

Verges Yes, I thank God, I am as honest as any man living, that is an old man, and no honester than I.

Dogberry Comparisons are odorous *palabras*, neighbour Verges.

Leonato Neighbours, you are tedious.

Dogberry It pleases your worship to say so, but we are the poor Duke's officers. But truly, for mine own part, if I were as tedious as a king I could find in my heart to bestow it all of your worship.

Leonato All thy tediousness on me, ah?

Dogberry Yea, an 'twere a thousand pound more than 'tis, for I hear as good exclamation on your worship as of any man in the city, and though I be but a poor man, I am glad to hear it.

Verges And so am I.

Leonato I would fain know what you have to say.

Verges Marry, sir, our Watch tonight, excepting your worship's presence, ha' ta'en a couple of as arrant knaves as any in Messina.

Dogberry A good old man, sir, he will be talking. As they say, "When the age is in, the wit is out." God help us, it is a world to see! Well said, i' faith, neighbour Verges. Well, God's a good man. An two men ride of a horse, one must ride behind. An honest soul, i'faith, sir, by my troth he is, as ever broke bread. But God is to be worshipped, all men are not alike. Alas, good neighbour.

Leonato Indeed neighbour, he comes too short of you.

Dogberry Gifts that God gives.

Leonato I must leave you.

Dogberry One word, sir. Our Watch, sir, have indeed comprehended two aspicious persons, and we would have them this morning examined before your worship.

Leonato Take their examination yourself and bring it me. I am now in great haste, as it may appear unto you.

Dogberry It shall be suffigance.

Leonato Drink some wine ere you go. Fare you well.

8 **Goodman:** a label such as 'Mr' today, given to men who were the next step down from a gentleman
9 **blunt:** he means 'sharp'
10–11 **honest as the skin between his brows:** refers to proverb 'everyone's fault is written on his forehead'
14 **odorous:** he means 'odious'
14 ***palabras*:** 'words' in Spanish – may refer to '*poco palabras*' ('few words'), a popular phrase at the time
18 **tedious:** he misunderstands 'tedious' for a word suggesting he is rich
22 **exclamation:** he means 'acclamation': praise
26 **I would fain know:** I'd really like to know
27 **excepting:** he means 'respecting'
28 **ha' ta'en:** have arrested
28 **arrant knaves:** hardened criminals
33 **An:** if
37 **he comes too short of you:** isn't your equal (intended ironically)
40 **comprehended:** he means 'apprehended': arrested
41 **aspicious:** he means 'suspicious' in the sense of them being suspected of a crime
42 **examined:** questioned
45 **suffigance:** he means 'sufficient'
46 **ere:** before

SHAKESPEARE'S WORLD

Slander, shame and reputation

In this scene, Claudio publicly shames Hero by accusing her of not being a virgin. In Shakespeare's time, women were expected to be obedient to their fathers and husbands and also chaste. To be chaste meant a woman should only have sex when married, and always be faithful to her husband. If an unmarried woman was not chaste, it reflected badly on her and on her father. As the head of the household, a father had to provide for the whole household; family and servants. He was also expected to make sure everyone in the household behaved properly.

Claudio refuses to marry Hero because he thinks she has been unchaste. By publicly slandering her, Claudio brings shame on her and her family. Leonato's reaction shows how serious this was. Shame was a type of exclusion; people were no longer treated by their community as they had been. It affected more than just their social life. Once a person's honour was questioned in one part of their life, people might doubt their honour in other areas and refuse, for example, to do business with them. Slander against a woman's chastity could ruin her and her family. The Friar proposes that Hero pretend to be dead from the shame of the slander. This would have seemed a possible (if extreme) reaction to Shakespeare's audience. He wants her to be publicly vindicated. He also wants her married to Claudio, despite his slander.

Hero and Claudio kneel before the Friar, in the background (*l–r*) Ursula, Leonato, another friar, musician, Don John, Don Pedro and Borachio (mainly hidden), 2011.

1. Look carefully at the people in the background. Who is speaking and which of his speeches is it most likely to be? Support your answer with quotes from the text.
2. What does the positioning and body language of Don Pedro, Don John and Borachio suggest? Explain your answer.

l–r Helen Weir, Joseph Marcell, Ony Uhiara, Joe Caffrey, Paul Ginika Etuka, Philip Cumbus, Dai Pritchard, Matthew Pidgeon, Ewan Stewart

Enter a messenger.

Messenger My lord, they stay for you to give your daughter to her husband.

Leonato I'll wait upon them. I am ready.

[Exit Leonato with Messenger.]

Dogberry Go, good partner, go get you to Francis Seacole. Bid him bring his pen and inkhorn to the jail. We are now to examination these men.

Verges And we must do it wisely.

Dogberry We will spare for no wit, I warrant you. Here's that shall drive some of them to a non-come. Only get the learned writer to set down our excommunication, and meet me at the jail.

Exit both.

47 **they stay:** everyone's waiting
49 **wait upon:** come to
51 **inkhorn:** ink pot
52 **examination:** he means examine
54 **Here's that:** what we have here
55 **non-come:** he means *non plus*, from the French for confusion
56 **excommunication:** he means 'examination'

Director's Note, 3.5

- ✔ Dogberry and Verges go to Leonato's house to tell him about the arrest of Borachio and Conrade.
- ✔ Leonato is busy, just about to go to the wedding, and their story is confused. He tells them to question Borachio and Conrade themselves, without realising what has happened.
- ✔ How many mistakes are there in this scene?

ACT 4 SCENE 1

Enter Don Pedro, Don John, Leonato, Friar Francis, Claudio, Benedick, Hero, Beatrice, and Attendants.

Leonato Come Friar Francis, be brief, only to the plain form of marriage, and you shall recount their particular duties afterwards.

Friar You come hither, my lord, to marry this lady?

Claudio No.

Leonato To be married to her. Friar, you come to marry her.

Friar Lady, you come hither to be married to this Count?

Hero I do.

Friar If either of you know any inward impediment why you should not be conjoined, I charge you on your souls to utter it.

Claudio Know you any, Hero?

Hero None my lord.

Friar Know you any, Count?

Leonato I dare make his answer, none.

Claudio O, what men dare do! What men may do! What men daily do, not knowing what they do!

Benedick How now? Interjections! Why then, some be of laughing, as, ah, ha, he.

Claudio Stand thee by, Friar. *[To Leonato.]* Father, by your leave,
Will you with free and unconstrainèd soul
Give me this maid your daughter?

Leonato As freely, son, as God did give her me.

1 **plain form:** brief version
2 **recount:** explain
9 **inward impediment:** secret obstacle
10 **conjoined:** married
10 **charge:** instruct
18 **Interjections:** interruptions
19 **as:** for example
20 **Stand thee by:** move aside
20 **by your leave:** excuse me
21 **with free and unconstrainèd soul:** with a clear conscience

A

A **Beatrice, Margaret, Hero, Leonato, with the Friar and two other friars in the background, 2011.**

B **Benedick, Margaret, Ursula, Beatrice and Hero, 2004.**

1 In both productions Hero is on the floor. Look carefully at the clues in the text. Is it more likely she collapsed, or that Claudio threw her to the floor? Quote to support your answer.

2 In Photo A Leonato has just spoken. Which line do you think he said? Explain your answer.

A Eve Best, Lisa McGrillis, Ony Uhiara, Joseph Marcell; ***B*** Josie Lawrence, Joy Richardson, Lucy Campbell, Yolanda Vazquez, Mariah Gale

B

Claudio
And what have I to give you back, whose worth
May counterpoise this rich and precious gift?

Don Pedro
Nothing, unless you render her again.

Claudio
Sweet Prince, you learn me noble thankfulness.
There Leonato, take her back again.
Give not this rotten orange to your friend,
She's but the sign and semblance of her honour.
Behold how like a maid she blushes here!
O what authority and show of truth
Can cunning sin cover itself withal!
Comes not that blood, as modest evidence,
To witness simple virtue? Would you not swear,
All you that see her, that she were a maid
By these exterior shows? But she is none.
She knows the heat of a luxurious bed.
Her blush is guiltiness, not modesty.

Leonato
What do you mean, my lord?

Claudio
Not to be married,
Not to knit my soul to an approvèd wanton.

Leonato
Dear my lord, if you in your own proof,
Have vanquished the resistance of her youth
And made defeat of her virginity —

Claudio
I know what you would say. If I have known her,
You will say, she did embrace me as a husband,
And so extenuate the 'forehand sin.
No Leonato, I never tempted her with word too large,
But as a brother to his sister, showed
Bashful sincerity and comely love.

Hero
And seemed I ever otherwise to you?

Claudio
Out on thee! Seeming! I will write against it.
You seem to me as Diane in her orb,
As chaste as is the bud ere it be blown.
But you are more intemperate in your blood
Than Venus, or those pamp'red animals
That rage in savage sensuality.

Hero
Is my lord well, that he doth speak so wide?

Leonato
Sweet Prince, why speak not you?

Don Pedro
What should I speak?
I stand dishonoured that have gone about
To link my dear friend to a common stale.

Leonato
Are these things spoken, or do I but dream?

Don John
Sir, they are spoken, and these things are true.

Benedick
[Aside.] This looks not like a nuptial.

Hero
True? O God!

Claudio
Leonato, stand I here? Is this the Prince? Is this the

---

25 **counterpoise:** balance, equal
26 **render her again:** give her back
27 **learn me:** teach me
29 **rotten orange:** oranges can look good on the outside and be rotten inside
30 **She's but the sign and semblance of her honour:** she looks virtuous, but she isn't
31 **maid:** virgin
32 **authority and show of truth:** convincing pretence
33 **withal:** with
34–5 **Comes not that blood … simple virtue:** don't her blushes look like evidence of her virtue
37 **these exterior shows:** her behaviour
38 **She knows the heat of a luxurious bed:** she's had sex with a man
41 **an approvèd wanton:** a woman known to be sexually promiscuous
42 **your own proof:** your testing of her virtue
43 **vanquished:** defeated
45 **known her:** had sex with her
47 **extenuate:** excuse
47 **the 'forehand sin:** having sex before the wedding
48 **word too large:** improper suggestions
50 **comely:** appropriate
52 **write against it:** publicly show otherwise
53 **Diane in her orb:** the goddess of chastity, as the moon, turning in the sky above
54 **the bud ere it be blown:** the rosebud before it opens
55 **more intemperate in your blood:** more sexual and passionate
56 **Venus:** the goddess of love
56–7 **pamp'red animals … sensuality:** creatures who do nothing but have sex all the time
58 **wide:** wide of the mark; inaccurately
60 **gone about:** made the effort
61 **common stale:** cheap prostitute
64 **nuptial:** wedding

Working Cut – text for experiment

Claudio Stand thee by, Friar. Father, by your leave,
Will you with free and unconstrainèd soul
Give me this maid your daughter?
Leonato As freely, son, as God did give her me.
Claudio And what have I to give you back, whose worth
May counterpoise this rich and precious gift?
Don Pedro Nothing, unless you render her again.
Claudio Sweet Prince, you learn me noble thankfulness.
There Leonato, take her back again.
Give not this rotten orange to your friend,
Leonato What do you mean, my lord?
Claudio Not to be married,
Not to knit my soul to an approvèd wanton.
Leonato Dear my lord, if you in your own proof,
Have vanquished the resistance of her youth
And made defeat of her virginity –
Claudio No Leonato, I never tempted her with word too large,
But as a brother to his sister, showed
Bashful sincerity and comely love.
Hero And seemed I ever otherwise to you?
Claudio Out on thee! Seeming! I will write against it.
You seem to me as Diane in her orb,
As chaste as is the bud ere it be blown.
But you are more intemperate in your blood
Than Venus, or those pamp'red animals
That rage in savage sensuality.
Hero Is my lord well, that he doth speak so wide?
Leonato Sweet Prince, why speak not you?
Don Pedro What should I speak?
I stand dishonoured that have gone about
To link my dear friend to a common stale
Benedick *[Aside.]* This looks not like a nuptial.
Claudio Let me but move one question to your daughter,
And by that fatherly and kindly power
That you have in her, bid her answer truly.
Leonato I charge thee do so, as thou art my child.
Claudio What man was he talked with you yesternight,
Out at your window betwixt twelve and one?
Now, if you are a maid, answer to this.
Hero I talked with no man at that hour my lord.
Don Pedro Why then you are no maiden. Leonato,
I am sorry you must hear. Upon my honour,
Myself, my brother, and this grievèd Count
Did see her, hear her, at that hour last night
Talk with a ruffian at her chamber window,
Who hath indeed, most like a liberal villain,
Confessed the vile encounters they have had
A thousand times in secret.
Claudio O Hero! What a Hero hadst thou been
If half thy outward graces had been placed
About thy thoughts and counsels of thy heart?
But fare thee well, most foul, most fair, farewell,
Leonato Hath no man's dagger here a point for me?

FROM THE REHEARSAL ROOM...

POINTING ON NAMES AND PRONOUNS

In groups of six read the *Working Cut*.

- Decide who will read each part. They are: Leonato, Hero, Friar, Claudio, Benedick and Don Pedro. Sit facing each other.
- Read through the scene and each time your character says a pronoun or a proper name, point at who or what you are talking to or about (e.g. 'my', 'your', 'our', or the characters' names …)
- Make sure you really do point at a definite person or place.
- If a character refers to somebody outside of the group of characters, point away from the group.

1 Are there any patterns in the pointing?
2 What does this scene tell us about Claudio?
3 How does Hero respond to the accusation?
4 How does Leonato respond to the information about his daughter?

- Now read the *Working Cut* again. This time, before you say your line, say aloud one word that really stood out from the previous character's line.
- Write down the words that were repeated aloud.
- Divide the words into two groups: words that shame and words that defend Hero.
- Discuss what you notice about the different groups of words.

5 How do the words sound?
6 What emotions do the words suggest?
7 Can you describe how Hero must feel at the end of this scene?

Prince's brother?
Is this face Hero's? Are our eyes our own?

Leonato All this is so, but what of this, my lord?

Claudio Let me but move one question to your daughter,
And by that fatherly and kindly power
That you have in her, bid her answer truly.

Leonato I charge thee do so, as thou art my child.

Hero O, God defend me, how am I beset!
What kind of catechising call you this?

Claudio To make you answer truly to your name.

Hero Is it not Hero? Who can blot that name
With any just reproach?

Claudio Marry that can Hero,
Hero itself can blot out Hero's virtue.
What man was he talked with you yesternight,
Out at your window betwixt twelve and one?
Now, if you are a maid, answer to this.

Hero I talked with no man at that hour my lord.

Don Pedro Why then you are no maiden. Leonato,
I am sorry you must hear. Upon my honour,
Myself, my brother, and this grievèd Count
Did see her, hear her, at that hour last night
Talk with a ruffian at her chamber window,
Who hath indeed, most like a liberal villain,
Confessed the vile encounters they have had
A thousand times in secret.

Don John Fie, fie, they are not to be named my lord,
Not to be spoke of.
There is not chastity enough in language
Without offence to utter them. Thus, pretty lady,
I am sorry for thy much misgovernment.

Claudio O Hero! What a Hero hadst thou been
If half thy outward graces had been placed
About thy thoughts and counsels of thy heart?
But fare thee well, most foul, most fair, farewell,
Thou pure impiety and impious purity.
For thee I'll lock up all the gates of love,
And on my eyelids shall conjecture hang,
To turn all beauty into thoughts of harm,
And never shall it more be gracious.

Leonato Hath no man's dagger here a point for me?

[Hero faints.]

Beatrice Why how now cousin, wherefore sink you down?

Don John Come, let us go. These things, come thus to light,
Smother her spirits up.

[Exit Don Pedro, Don John, and Claudio.]

69 **move:** ask
70 **kindly power:** power you have over her because she's your child
73 **beset:** attacked on all sides
74 **catechising:** questioning (refers to the Elizabethan Christian catechism, a set of questions that must be answered truthfully)
75 **answer truly to your name:** the first question of the Elizabethan catechism was 'What is your name?'
76 **blot:** stain
77 **just reproach:** fair accusation
86 **grievèd:** wronged (because he wooed her for Claudio)
89 **liberal:** unrestrained
96 **much misgovernment:** hugely uncontrolled behaviour
98–9 **If half thy outward graces ... thy heart:** if your morals were even as half as good as you look lovely
101 **Thou pure impiety and impious purity:** you pure sinner and sinful innocent
102 **For thee:** because of you
102 **all the gates of love:** all openness to love
103 **on my eyelids shall conjecture hang:** I'll always look suspiciously
105 **gracious:** attractive
106 **Hath no man's dagger here a point for me?:** someone kill me now
108 **come thus to light:** revealed in this way
109 **Smother her spirits up:** have overcome her

Beatrice, Ursula, Hero and the Friar, 2011.

1 Why is Hero on the ground now? Give reasons for your answer.

2 Who are the three women looking at, and why do they have these facial expressions? Quote from the text to support your answer.

Eve Best, Helen Weir, Ony Uhiara, Joe Caffrey

Actor's view

Mariah Gale
Hero, 2004

A friend who came to see the play said that she always found it frustrating that a lot of the female characters in Shakespeare don't really speak out very much in their own defence, she felt, and that Hero was one of those characters. But then watching it she felt that actually that silence can sometimes be a strength and if Hero had kicked up a fuss in the wedding perhaps it would have been taken as guilt. I don't know, I feel like she doesn't feel that she has to explain any more than the simple truth. And in a way you could see that as a weakness because I suppose she's never had to really speak out and she's never had a situation before where people have turned against her. And so I think partly she might be tongue-tied and stunned by what's happening, but I also think it's an important lesson for her that it comes down to it and she does have to put forward her argument in her own defence to her father.

She's in such a lovely world and then that gets shattered in the most shocking way and I think that in the line, 'Oh God defend me, how am I beset?' she's asking for help from God because she doesn't get help from anywhere else. It's really interesting that Beatrice doesn't speak until Claudio's gone, she doesn't dare, none of the women do. In a sense, that might be because when someone's screaming abuse at you the best thing to do sometimes is to just listen until they've rid themselves of rage, then you can talk rationally with them and perhaps that's what's going on. Because they'd have probably got into a fantastic argument if Beatrice had said what she really felt, and she can't really let that out until she's with Benedick, who she trusts enough at this point to be able to vent and say the most extreme things.

Actor's view

Penelope Beaumont
Leonato, 2004

'Could she here deny
The story that is printed in her blood?'

Her colour is rushing to her face. Now, I'm taking that as an admission of her guilt, but for her, it's happening because she's so upset and doesn't know what's happening to her. She can't understand. She's so frightened of her father and how on earth is she going to get out of this nightmare. But for him it's, 'Look at her, she's blushing' and that's the physical embodiment of her wrong. So,

'Could she here deny
The story that is printed in her blood?
Do not live, Hero, do not ope thine eyes.
For did I think thou wouldst not quickly die,
Thought I thy spirits were stronger than thy shames,
Myself would on the rearward of reproaches
Strike at thy life.'

Benedick How doth the lady?

Beatrice Dead, I think. Help, uncle!
Hero, why Hero! Uncle, Signior Benedick, Friar!

Leonato O Fate, take not away thy heavy hand,
Death is the fairest cover for her shame
That may be wished for.

Beatrice *[Hero stirs.]* How now, cousin Hero?

Friar Have comfort, lady.

Leonato Dost thou look up?

Friar Yea, wherefore should she not?

Leonato Wherefore? Why, doth not every earthly thing
Cry shame upon her? Could she here deny
The story that is printed in her blood?
Do not live, Hero, do not ope thine eyes.
For did I think thou wouldst not quickly die,
Thought I thy spirits were stronger than thy shames,
Myself would on the rearward of reproaches
Strike at thy life. Grieved I, I had but one?
Chid I for that at frugal nature's frame?
O one too much by thee. Why had I one?
Why ever wast thou lovely in my eyes?
Why had I not with charitable hand
Took up a beggar's issue at my gates,
Who smirchèd thus and mired with infamy,
I might have said, "No part of it is mine.
This shame derives itself from unknown loins".
But mine, and mine I loved, and mine I praised,
And mine that I was proud on, mine so much
That I myself was to myself not mine,
Valuing of her. Why she, O she is fall'n
Into a pit of ink, that the wide sea
Hath drops too few to wash her clean again,
And salt too little which may season give
To her foul tainted flesh!

Benedick Sir, sir, be patient. For my part, I am so attired in wonder, I know not what to say.

Beatrice O, on my soul, my cousin is belied!

Benedick Lady, were you her bedfellow last night?

Beatrice No, truly, not, although until last night,
I have this twelvemonth been her bedfellow.

Leonato Confirmed, confirmed! O, that is stronger made
Which was before barred up with ribs of iron.
Would the two princes lie? And Claudio lie,
Who loved her so, that, speaking of her foulness,
Washed it with tears? Hence from her, let her die!

Friar Hear me a little,
For I have only been silent so long,

113 **take not away thy heavy hand:** let her die

118 **Dost thou look up?:** do you dare turn your eyes to heaven for help?

121 **printed in her blood:** two meanings: 1) shown by her blushes; 2) part of her nature

123 **For did I think:** because if I thought

124 **Thought I:** if I thought

125–6 **Myself would on the rearward ... thy life:** I'd kill you myself

126 **Grieved I, I had but one?:** did I regret having just one child?

127 **Chid I for that at frugal nature's frame?:** did I wish nature had given me more?

128 **one too much by thee:** you were one too many

129 **wast:** were

130 **had I not:** didn't I

131 **Took up a beggar's issue:** adopted a beggar's child

132 **Who smirchèd thus and mired with infamy:** So when they did this awful thing

134 **derives itself from unknown loins:** is the fault of the birth parents

137–8 **That I myself ... Valuing of her:** that I forgot myself in caring for her

141–2 **And salt too little ... tainted flesh:** nothing can preserve her reputation (salt was used to stop meat from rotting)

143–4 **attired in wonder:** amazed

145 **is belied:** is slandered

146 **were you her bedfellow:** did you share her bed (sharing beds with family of the same sex was common at the time)

153 **Hence from her:** leave her alone

Benedick, Beatrice and Hero, 2008.

Compare this photo with those from the 2004 and 2011 productions on page 74.

1 Explain at least two differences between the 2008 production and the other two.

2 Explain at least two similarities between the 2008 production and the other two.

3 What will be the effect on the audience of involving Benedick in caring for Hero this early in the scene?

Bill Buckhurst, Kirsty Besterman, Natasha Magigi

SHAKESPEARE'S WORLD

Friars

Friars make regular appearances in the plays of the time. They were part of the Roman Catholic Church, more like monks than priests, but they lived and worked amongst the people. They could conduct marriage ceremonies, give advice and hear confessions. Because at this time Catholicism was illegal in England, friars only appear in plays set in other countries, or at a previous time in English history. Many members of the audience would regard Catholics, and therefore friars, with suspicion. They were also often thought of as being greedy and nosey. Playwrights of the time often used friars as characters to be made fun of, or even killed. In Shakespeare's plays, though, they are treated with more sympathy. However, whenever they appear, they take an active part in other characters' lives. This is often described as 'meddling'. The Friar in this play meddles after the failed wedding of Act 4 Scene 1. He suggests an elaborate plot, involving a fake death, which may lead to a happy ending. The same goes for the most famous of Shakespeare's friars, Friar Lawrence in *Romeo and Juliet*, although his meddling has a tragic end. An audience seeing a friar in Shakespeare's plays, then, would have a good idea what to expect.

And given way unto this course of fortune,
By noting of the lady. I have marked
A thousand blushing apparitions
To start into her face, a thousand innocent shames
In angel whiteness beat away those blushes.
And in her eye there hath appeared a fire
To burn the errors that these princes hold
Against her maiden truth. Call me a fool,
Trust not my reading nor my observations,
Which with experimental seal doth warrant
The tenor of my book. Trust not my age,
My reverence, calling, nor divinity,
If this sweet lady lie not guiltless here,
Under some biting error.

Leonato Friar, it cannot be.
Thou seest that all the grace that she hath left
Is that she will not add to her damnation
A sin of perjury. She not denies it.
Why seek'st thou then to cover with excuse
That which appears in proper nakedness?

Friar Lady, what man is he you are accused of?

Hero They know that do accuse me, I know none.
If I know more of any man alive
Than that which maiden modesty doth warrant,
Let all my sins lack mercy. O my father,
Prove you that any man with me conversed
At hours unmeet, or that I yesternight
Maintained the change of words with any creature,
Refuse me, hate me, torture me to death!

Friar There is some strange misprision in the princes.

Benedick Two of them have the very bent of honour,
And if their wisdoms be misled in this,
The practice of it lives in John the Bastard,
Whose spirits toil in frame of villainies.

Leonato I know not. If they speak but truth of her,
These hands shall tear her. If they wrong her honour,
The proudest of them shall well hear of it.
Time hath not yet so dried this blood of mine,
Nor age so eat up my invention,
Nor Fortune made such havoc of my means,
Nor my bad life reft me so much of friends,
But they shall find, awaked in such a kind
Both strength of limb and policy of mind,
Ability in means, and choice of friends,
To quit me of them throughly.

Friar Pause awhile
And let my counsel sway you in this case.
Your daughter here the princes left for dead,
Let her awhile be secretly kept in,
And publish it that she is dead indeed.

156 **given way unto this course of fortune:** let things go along like this
157 **By noting of the lady:** to watch Hero's reaction
157 **marked:** noticed
158–60 **A thousand blushing apparitions ... beat away those blushes:** she blushes many times, only to go pale because she knows she is innocent of the crimes she is accused of
162 **her maiden truth:** the truth of her virginity
165–6 **with experimental seal ... tenor of my book:** which confirms all I have learned from books
167 **divinity:** being a clergyman
169 **biting:** painful, damaging
173 **perjury:** swearing something that isn't true
175 **proper nakedness:** plain truth
179 **warrant:** permit
180 **lack mercy:** go unforgiven
182 **hours unmeet:** an unsuitable time
183 **Maintained the change of words:** spoke
184 **Refuse:** disown
185 **misprision:** misunderstanding
186 **have the very bent of honour:** are honourable men
188 **The practice of it lives in:** it's because of
189 **Whose spirits toil in frame of villainies:** who is constantly planning evil deeds
192 **The proudest:** the most important
194 **invention:** ability to plan
195 **Nor Fortune made such havoc of my means:** I've not been made poor by chance
196 **reft me so much of:** taken away so many
197 **in such a kind:** if she is slandered
201 **counsel:** advice
203 **secretly kept in:** hidden
204 **publish it:** tell everyone

Leonato, Beatrice, Hero, Ursula and the Friar, while the Friar explains his plan, 2011.

1 List each character shown, and say who each one is looking at.

2 Explain the logic behind each actor's choice about who to look at.

Joseph Marcell, Eve Best, Ony Uhiara, Helen Weir, Joe Caffrey

Actor's view

Yolanda Vazquez
Beatrice, 2004

When the ceremony is about to start, before they go in, there is this huge shock for all of them. I think that Beatrice, during all of this, doesn't speak at all because she is stunned by what she's hearing. I think that she's thinking, 'This is all lies. They have no proof. How dare they? How dare they? How have they not come to the house beforehand? How dare they do this in public with no proof whatsoever.' And I think that it's that frustration, and not being able to stand up for her nearest and dearest, and not being able to stand up for what she knows is true. What they're saying is a lie, it's that frustration that makes her weep. It's that frustration that Benedick then sees the release of (which is her weeping afterwards in the church). And that's why one of her first comments afterwards is, 'O that I were a man', and I think she absolutely, one hundred percent means that. If she were a man, if she had been born male those men would have had a challenge from her, but she can't do that and I think that keeps her dumb and frustrated. There is nothing that she can do, absolutely nothing, it has to be left to the others; it has to be left, unfortunately, to the two older men and the Friar.

Actor's view

Penelope Beaumont
Leonato, 2004

At the end of the wedding scene the Friar says, 'if everyone thinks she's dead then they will think well of her', because you never know what you've had until you've lost it, is really what he's saying. You don't value what you have until it's gone. And I think that, for me, is the moment where Hero has told me absolutely that she's innocent. I've let that possibility enter my heart, and then when the Friar says, 'you must value what you've got while it's there', my Leonato realises that he's in danger of doing that himself, of losing Hero, and just how dreadful that would be. And so I kneel down to her and take her hand and that's, I hope for the audience, the start of seeing that he does believe her.

Maintain a mourning ostentation,
And on your family's old monument
Hang mournful epitaphs, and do all rites
That appertain unto a burial.

Leonato What shall become of this? What will this do?

Friar Marry, this well carried, shall on her behalf,
Change slander to remorse. That is some good.
But not for that dream I on this strange course,
But on this travail look for greater birth.
She dying, as it must be so maintained,
Upon the instant that she was accused,
Shall be lamented, pitied, and excused
Of every hearer. For it so falls out,
That what we have we prize not to the worth
Whiles we enjoy it. But being lacked and lost,
Why then we rack the value, then we find
The virtue that possession would not show us
Whiles it was ours. So will it fare with Claudio.
When he shall hear she died upon his words,
The idea of her life shall sweetly creep
Into his study of imagination.
And every lovely organ of her life
Shall come apparelled in more precious habit,
More moving, delicate, and full of life,
Into the eye and prospect of his soul
Than when she lived indeed. Then shall he mourn,
If ever love had interest in his liver,
And wish he had not so accusèd her.
No, though he thought his accusation true,
Let this be so, and doubt not but success
Will fashion the event in better shape
Than I can lay it down in likelihood.
But if all aim but this be levelled false,
The supposition of the lady's death
Will quench the wonder of her infamy.
And if it sort not well, you may conceal her,
As best befits her wounded reputation,
In some reclusive and religious life,
Out of all eyes, tongues, minds and injuries.

Benedick Signor Leonato, let the Friar advise you.
And though you know my inwardness and love
Is very much unto the Prince and Claudio,
Yet, by mine honour, I will deal in this
As secretly and justly as your soul
Should with your body.

Leonato Being that I flow in grief,
The smallest twine may lead me.

Friar 'Tis well consented. Presently away,
For to strange sores strangely they strain the cure.
Come lady, die to live. This wedding day
Perhaps is but prolonged, have patience and endure.

Exit all except Beatrice and Benedick.

205 **mourning ostentation:** obvious show of grief
206 **monument:** tomb
207 **epitaphs:** poems mourning the dead
207 **rites:** ceremonies
208 **appertain unto:** are needed for
210 **Marry:** by Mary (Christ's mother)
212 **dream I on this strange course:** have I worked out this complicated plan
213 **travail:** effort
217 **falls out:** happens
218–9 **we prize not to the worth Whiles we enjoy it:** we don't value enough while we have it
219 **being lacked and lost:** when we lose it
220 **we rack:** we stretch, drive up
220–22 **we find The virtue that … it was ours:** we understand its worth, which we didn't while we owned it
222 **So will it fare with:** that's what will happen to
225 **his study of imagination:** his thoughts
226 **organ:** here used to mean 'part'
227 **apparelled:** dressed
227 **habit:** clothes
229 **the eye and prospect of his soul:** his mind's eye
231 **his liver:** thought at the time to be where love began
233 **though:** even though
236 **lay it down in likelihood:** plan it
237 **be levelled false:** comes to nothing
239 **quench the wonder of her infamy:** stop all talk of her disgrace
240 **sort not:** doesn't turn out
240–42 **you may conceal her … and religious life:** you can send her to a nunnery
245 **inwardness:** friendship and loyalty
249 **Being that:** because
250 **smallest twine:** thinnest string
251 **Presently away:** let's go
252 **For to strange sores … the cure:** desperate ills need desperate cures
254 **Perhaps is but prolonged:** may just be postponed

Beatrice and Benedick, 2011.

Where in the text on page 85 is the exact point the photograph was taken? Give reasons for your answer.

Eve Best, Charles Edwards

Working Cut – text for experiment

Benedick I do love nothing in the world so well as you. Is not that strange?
Beatrice As strange as the thing I know not. It were as possible for me to say I loved nothing so well as you. But believe me not, and yet I lie not. I confess nothing, nor I deny nothing. – I am sorry for my cousin.
Benedick By my sword Beatrice thou lovest me.
Beatrice Do not swear by it and eat it.
Benedick I will swear by it that you love me, and I will make him eat it that says I love not you.
Beatrice Why then, God forgive me.
Benedick What offence, sweet Beatrice?
Beatrice You have stayed me in a happy hour, I was about to protest I loved you.
Benedick And do it with all thy heart.
Beatrice I love you with so much of my heart that none is left to protest.
Benedick Come, bid me do anything for thee.
Beatrice Kill Claudio.
Benedick Ha, not for the wide world.
Beatrice You kill me to deny it, farewell. *[She starts to leave.]*
Benedick Tarry sweet Beatrice.
Beatrice I am gone, though I am here. There is no love in you. Nay I pray you, let me go.
Benedick We'll be friends first.
Beatrice You dare easier be friends with me than fight with mine enemy.
Benedick Is Claudio thine enemy?
Beatrice Is he not approved in the height a villain, that hath slandered, scorned, dishonoured my kinswoman? O God, that I were a man! I would eat his heart in the marketplace.
Benedick Hear me, Beatrice –
Beatrice Sweet Hero, she is wronged, she is slandered, she is undone.
Benedick Beat –
Beatrice I cannot be a man with wishing, therefore I will die a woman with grieving.
Benedick Tarry good Beatrice, by this hand I love thee.
Beatrice Use it for my love some other way than swearing by it.
Benedick Think you in your soul the Count Claudio hath wronged Hero?
Beatrice Yea, as sure as I have a thought, or a soul.
Benedick Enough, I am engaged, I will challenge him.

FROM THE REHEARSAL ROOM...

POINTING ON PRONOUNS

- This is the same activity as on page 76. Re-read the instructions.
- In pairs, decide who will read Beatrice and Benedick.
- Read through the *Working Cut*, pointing on the pronouns or proper names.

1 Are there any patterns in the pointing?
2 What does this scene tell us about how Beatrice feels?

MAGNETS

- Now stand opposite each other. Read the *Working Cut* again, but this time take one step forward if you think your character is leading, one step backwards if you feel your character is retreating or two steps forward if your character is following.

3 Who takes the lead, Benedick or Beatrice? Explain your answer.

Benedick Lady Beatrice, have you wept all this while?

Beatrice Yea, and I will weep a while longer.

Benedick I will not desire that.

Beatrice You have no reason, I do it freely.

Benedick Surely I do believe your fair cousin is wronged.

Beatrice Ah, how much might the man deserve of me that would right her!

Benedick Is there any way to show such friendship?

Beatrice A very even way, but no such friend.

Benedick May a man do it?

Beatrice It is a man's office, but not yours.

Benedick I do love nothing in the world so well as you. Is not that strange?

Beatrice As strange as the thing I know not. It were as possible for me to say I loved nothing so well as you. But believe me not, and yet I lie not. I confess nothing, nor I deny nothing. — I am sorry for my cousin.

Benedick By my sword Beatrice thou lovest me.

Beatrice Do not swear by it and eat it.

Benedick I will swear by it that you love me, and I will make him eat it that says I love not you.

Beatrice Will you not eat your word?

Benedick With no sauce that can be devised to it. I protest I love thee.

Beatrice Why then, God forgive me.

Benedick What offence, sweet Beatrice?

Beatrice You have stayed me in a happy hour, I was about to protest I loved you.

Benedick And do it with all thy heart.

Beatrice I love you with so much of my heart that none is left to protest.

Benedick Come, bid me do anything for thee.

Beatrice Kill Claudio.

Benedick Ha, not for the wide world.

Beatrice You kill me to deny it, farewell. *[She starts to leave.]*

Benedick Tarry sweet Beatrice.

Beatrice I am gone, though I am here. There is no love in you. Nay I pray you, let me go.

Benedick Beatrice —

Beatrice In faith I will go.

258 **have no reason:** don't need to

260–1 **might the man deserve of me that would right her:** what I would owe the man who would prove her innocence

263 **even:** clear, obvious

265 **office:** job

268 **As strange as the thing I know not:** I can't think of anything as strange

272 **By my sword:** said to swear a person is telling the truth

273 **eat it:** go back on his word

277 **devised to it:** made to flavour it well

280 **stayed me in a happy hour:** stopped me just in time

289 **Tarry:** wait

290 **I am gone, though I am here:** I'm here in body, but not in spirit

Benedick and Beatrice from line 290 to the end of this scene, 2004.

1 Which order do you think these three photos were taken in? Give reasons for your answer.

2 Pick one phrase or line to be the caption for each photo, and give reasons for your answer.

Josie Lawrence,
Yolanda Vazquez

FROM THE REHEARSAL ROOM...

LOVE ON THE LINE

This is a repeat of the activity on pages 10, 34, 50 and 58. Look back at the instructions.

- Working in small groups, read the *Working Cut* on page 84. Pick readers for Beatrice and Benedick. The rest of you are 'listeners'.
- As the readers work through the *Working Cut*, the 'listeners' should repeat, as a whisper, any declarations of love.

1 Where is Beatrice on the line? Quote from the text to support your answer.

2 Where is Benedick on the line? Quote from the text to support your answer.

- Stand in the places on the line, and compare your answers with other groups. Use your quotes to support your views.

3 Record your answers, and those that the majority of the class agree on.

Benedick We'll be friends first.

Beatrice You dare easier be friends with me than fight with mine enemy.

Benedick Is Claudio thine enemy?

Beatrice Is he not approved in the height a villain, that hath slandered, scorned, dishonoured my kinswoman? O that I were a man! What, bear her in hand until they come to take hands, and then with public accusation, uncovered slander, unmitigated rancour — O God, that I were a man! I would eat his heart in the marketplace.

Benedick Hear me, Beatrice —

Beatrice Talk with a man out at a window! A proper saying!

Benedick Nay but Beatrice —

Beatrice Sweet Hero, she is wronged, she is slandered, she is undone.

Benedick Beat—

Beatrice Princes and counties! Surely a princely testimony, a goodly Count. Count Comfect, a sweet gallant surely. O that I were a man for his sake! Or that I had any friend would be a man for my sake! But manhood is melted into curtsies, valour into compliment, and men are only turned into tongue, and trim ones too. He is now as valiant as Hercules that only tells a lie, and swears it. I cannot be a man with wishing, therefore I will die a woman with grieving.

Benedick Tarry good Beatrice, by this hand I love thee.

Beatrice Use it for my love some other way than swearing by it.

Benedick Think you in your soul the Count Claudio hath wronged Hero?

Beatrice Yea, as sure as I have a thought, or a soul.

Benedick Enough, I am engaged, I will challenge him. I will kiss your hand, and so I leave you. By this hand, Claudio shall render me a dear account. As you hear of me, so think of me. Go comfort your cousin, I must say she is dead, and so farewell. *[Exit Benedick and Beatrice.]*

295–6 **You dare easier be friends with me than fight with mine enemy:** you're happy to be my friend, but not to fight my enemy
298 **approved in the height:** clearly
300 **bear her in hand:** lead her on
301 **to take hands:** to the wedding
302 **unmitigated rancour:** complete hatred
305 **A proper saying:** completely made up
311 **Comfect:** double meaning: 1) something sweet; 2) something made up
315 **only turned into tongue:** all talk
315 **trim:** elegant
316 **valiant:** brave
317 **swears it:** swears the lie is true
319 **by this hand:** said to swear a person is telling the truth
320 **Use it for my love ... swearing by it:** fight Claudio, then
324 **I am engaged:** I promise
326 **render me a dear account:** pay dearly for what he's done

Director's Note, 4.1

- ✔ Claudio refuses to marry Hero, publicly accusing her of being unfaithful.
- ✔ Don Pedro supports Claudio, Hero faints and he, Claudio and Don John leave.
- ✔ Leonato at first blames Hero, but the Friar persuades him she may be innocent, and to pretend she has died.
- ✔ Beatrice and Benedick are left together. They admit their love for one another, and reluctantly Benedick agrees to challenge Claudio to a duel.

Actor's view

Charles Edwards
Benedick, 2011

What he says, 'no, absolutely not, not for the whole wide world'. And then he listens to her, sees how upset she is, how fully and wholly she believes it with her soul that it needs to be addressed, and he says, 'alright, I'll do it'. Eve Best [Beatrice] was very much of the opinion that you shouldn't try to quell the laugh on 'kill Claudio', and I agree with her completely. They are just professing undying love to one another and then she says it, and of course you're going to laugh, whether with surprise or shock. And the [audience] are behind her as well, they're on her side, they want to see this guy – because they know it's all a plot – they want to see him get his comeuppance. I've read a lot about how to deal with that laugh but I think it's going to get a laugh, so why try and stop it? It's not to do with the delivery, it's to do with the line. But the moments preceding it are the tentative moments of them saying they love each other and those can be funny, they are rather fumbling and clumsy as it is for most of us. Laughter has been developing in the early part of that dialogue which I welcome because it's warm.

STUDY NOTES, 4.1

TIP

A good response

A good response may refer to effects on the character on stage and then to effects on people in the audience.

For example, the effect of this scene on Claudio is that Shakespeare shows him as feeling justified and satisfied in taking his revenge on the person he thinks has deceived and wronged him – Hero.

The effect on the audience is that Shakespeare shows Claudio as deceived – but by Don John and not Hero, and that Claudio has too easily believed what he has heard. He has done wrong to Hero by not trusting her or believing her.

TIP

Writing about drama

Sometimes Shakespeare creates dramatic tension by writing very little for an actor, even though the actor is on stage and hears and sees what others do and say, like Hero. This means the actor has to find a way of showing reactions without speaking. Commenting on how a part may be performed when there are no lines shows that you understand this aspect of performance.

1 Character and plot development

So far, the main action has been light-hearted and amusing. Now an ugly situation develops as a contrast.

1 Act 4 Scene 1 brings the tragic plot to the fore. Shakespeare makes the brutal scene more shocking by starting the scene with an exchange between Claudio, Leonato and the Friar which could be performed as a humorous contrast to what follows, or as a confusing and menacing build-up. Which way of performing it develops characters and plot more effectively? Support your answer by referring to what the characters say and how they might say it.

2 Which lines does Shakespeare write to indicate a gradual building up to Claudio's brutal rejection?

3 How does Shakespeare present Hero as an honest, innocent and vulnerable victim of Don John's wicked plan? Select words from the text to support what you say.

2 Characterisation and voice: dramatic language

In this scene, passions run high and strong feelings are expressed in strong language conveying anger and hurt – but also disbelief and amazement, as the evil plot works to destroy happiness and trust. It is through angry voices that much of this scene has an impact.

4 Choose three expressions that Shakespeare uses to convey Claudio's disgust and bitterness about Hero's imagined offence (lines 27–58).

5 What makes Don Pedro seem convinced about Hero's guilt and concerned about his own reputation, rather than trying to find out the truth? Think about what he says and how he says it (lines 26–92).

6 What details might suggest that Leonato is more concerned with his public reputation and honour than with his daughter's feelings? Look closely at what he says and how he says it (lines 120–201).

3 Themes and ideas

Shakespeare develops themes of guilt and innocence, trust and mistrust in the scene, with attitudes and ideas about women's virtue and suitability for marriage getting in the way of the truth.

7 What do you think Shakespeare shows as Claudio's cause of anger – disappointment, anger at being cheated or wounded pride? Look at lines 53–8, 98–106, and look back at Act 1 Scene 1 line 155 and Act 2 Scene 1 lines 166–7.

8 Hero doesn't defend herself. Does this suggest she is too shocked and hurt to reply or that she is too passive and naïve for her own good? Give reasons for your answer.

9 Why, do you think, does Shakespeare make Beatrice do so little in the first part of this scene when he has shown her previously to be confident and assertive?

10 In what ways are the various meanings of 'Nothing' important in the 'Much Ado' presented in this scene?

STUDY NOTES, 4.1

4 Performance

Actors and directors have lots of choice in making this scene effective. They may want to make Claudio seem so distressed by what he has heard that he can't control himself – which may make the audience sympathise with him. Or they may want to make him seem spoiled and arrogant, cruelly believing others and thinking the worst of Hero – which may make the audience dislike him and pity Hero more.

11 If you were advising the actor playing Claudio, would you advise him to play this scene coldly and unemotionally or with tearful and passionate anger? Look at lines 16–17, 24–5, 40–1, 53–8 and explain your choices.

12 Benedick has little dialogue in the first part of the scene (lines 18–19, 65 and 111). How might you advise the actor playing him to react to what he is seeing and hearing at these three points and between them?

13 How might the actor playing Hero react to the various stages of Claudio's attack upon her honour?

14 How do you think the actor playing the the Friar might present his plan – as a confident, wise, practical strategy or as a tentative best thing that can be done in the circumstances?

5 Contexts and responses

Different ages and different societies have different attitudes to reputation, to women and to marriage. This may lead to different responses to the scene here. Some may think Hero's silence is a sign of confidence – others may think it a sign of her lack of assertiveness, and a disadvantage.

15 Is the public humiliation and shame in this scene something to do with the time the play was written or set in, or could it occur in a community today?

16 Would a modern audience sympathise with any of Claudio's feelings and behaviour in this scene?

17 How may audiences respond differently to Leonato's reactions as Hero's father?

6 Reflecting on the scene

18 In what ways does Shakespeare make this scene a tragic contrast to the scenes that have gone before? Give evidence to support your answer.

19 How does Shakespeare present relationships between male and female characters in this scene?

20 How has your appreciation of this scene been enhanced by stage, screen or classroom performance?

USING THE VIDEO

Exploring interpretation and performance

If you have looked at the video extracts in the online version try these questions.

- The 2004 and 2011 productions create audience laughter at Benedick's 'Is that not strange?' and at 'Kill Claudio'. Do you think this way of playing the lines:
  - a) spoils the romantic and dramatic qualities of the script *or*
  - b) is along the lines that Shakespeare intended?

  You could view the 2011 clip of the wedding, to set the scene.
- How does the use of close-ups in the 2011 production affect your response to the scene compared with the presentation of the 2004 production?

TIP

Reflecting on the scene

Writing about dramatic techniques can be improved by linking to performance. Show how your understanding has been developed by seeing the text performed on stage or screen, or through performance of an aspect of the scene yourself or as part of a group.

A Dogberry (in legal robes), Verges, Conrade, a member of the Watch and Borachio, 2011.

B Borachio and two members of the Watch, 2008.

1. How have the two productions shown that Borachio (and Conrade in 2011) are prisoners?
2. Pick one of Dogberry's lines that could be used as a caption for Photo A, and give reasons for your choice.
3. Who do you think was speaking when Photo B was taken? Explain your choice.

A Paul Hunter, Adrian Hood, Marcus Griffiths, Paul Ginika Etuka, Joe Caffrey
B Mark Rice-Oxley, Christopher John Hall, Kirsty Besterman

ACT 4 SCENE 2

Enter Dogberry, Verges, the Sexton in legal robes, and the Watch, with Borachio and Conrade as prisoners.

Dogberry Is our whole dissembly appeared?

Verges O a stool and a cushion for the sexton.

Sexton *[He sits.]* Which be the malefactors?

Dogberry Marry that am I, and my partner.

Verges Nay that's certain. We have the exhibition to examine.

Sexton But which are the offenders that are to be examined? Let them come before Master Constable.

Dogberry Yea, marry, let them come before me. *[The Watch bring Borachio and Conrade forward.]* What is your name, friend?

Borachio Borachio.

Dogberry Pray write down "Borachio". Yours sirrah?

Conrade I am a gentleman sir, and my name is Conrade.

Dogberry Write down "master gentleman Conrade". Masters, do you serve God?

Conrade and Borachio Yea sir, we hope.

Dogberry Write down that they hope they serve God. And write God first, for God defend but God should go before such villains! Masters, it is proved already that you are little better than false knaves, and it will go near to be thought so shortly. How answer you for yourselves?

Conrade Marry, sir, we say we are none.

Dogberry A marvellous witty fellow, I assure you, but I will go about with him. Come you hither, sirrah. A word in your ear, sir. I say to you, it is thought you are false knaves.

Borachio Sir, I say to you, we are none.

Dogberry Well, stand aside. 'Fore God, they are both in a tale. Have you writ down that they are none?

Sexton Master Constable, you go not the way to examine. You must call forth the Watch that are their accusers.

Dogberry Yea, marry, that's the eftest way. Let the watch come forth. Masters, I charge you in the Prince's name, accuse these men.

Seacole(First Watchman) This man said, sir, that Don John, the Prince's brother, was a villain.

Dogberry Write down "Prince John a villain". Why, this is flat perjury, to call a Prince's brother villain.

Borachio Master Constable—

1 **dissembly:** he means 'assembly': group

2 **sexton:** a person who worked for the parish church

3 **malefactors:** evil-doers

4 **Marry:** by Mary (Christ's mother)

5 **the exhibition:** he means 'commission': official permission

11 **sirrah:** a way of saying 'sir' to someone to show contempt for them

17 **defend:** he means 'forfend': forbid

22–3 **go about with him:** get the better of him

23 **hither:** here

26 **they are both in a tale:** their stories agree

30 **eftest:** he means 'easiest'

Dogberry, at the end of the scene, 2011.

1 Quote from the text on page 91 to show that the Sexton is doing the writing down, not Dogberry.

2 In this production Dogberry stayed on stage as the others left, and this moment is shown in the photo. What, in the text, has prompted this last piece of business? Explain your answer.

Paul Hunter

Actor's view

Paul Hunter
Dogberry, 2011

At the end of one scene he's told by Leonato, who's very busy and can't be bothered with these two idiots, 'you can try these men, you can become the magistrate.' And I think that's the key thing. That's suddenly where, if it was the movie, he would have a fantasy moment of being this American lawyer in the courtroom. In my head that's what I think about. I think it's got to be that. This is his moment. He makes a complete pig's ear of it, of course, and it is complete chaos. If Shakespeare had created a really credible villain in Don John, you'd have had a much more serious Watch, a competent Watch. You know in a way, because the Watch are so ludicrous, that Don John can't get away with this. He's not like Iago [in Othello*]. If he was like Iago we would have to be very credible. You couldn't be a bunch of idiots or you'd never catch him. So, I think it's wonderful, the more we do the play, how Shakespeare merges these things together.*

And also how he extraordinarily puts a scene which is incredibly brutal, the shaming of Hero, which is sort of unwatchable to a modern audience immediately next to this ludicrous court scene. It's a really savage, brutal attack on this woman – it's brilliantly written and everything and then he has the ludicrous court scene. And I think that's what makes Shakespeare so experimental, genuinely experimental, because a lot of modern writers wouldn't do that. They'd go 'OK, we can have that scene, we can't put that scene next to that, not after what we've had.' Whereas Shakespeare goes 'we can do exactly that.' And also within the course of one scene, as he does later on, when it's been revealed to Don Pedro what went wrong, he then brings in this idiot again ... and that's why it's so extraordinary and I think a lot of modern writers wouldn't have the bravery to do that.

Dogberry Pray thee fellow, peace. I do not like thy look I promise thee.

Sexton What heard you him say else?

Second Watchman Marry, that he had received a thousand ducats of Don John for accusing the Lady Hero wrongfully.

Dogberry Flat burglary as ever was committed.

Verges Yea, by th' mass, that it is.

Sexton What else fellow?

Seacole And that Count Claudio did mean, upon his words, to disgrace Hero before the whole assembly, and not marry her.

Dogberry O villain! Thou wilt be condemned into everlasting redemption for this.

Sexton What else?

Seacole This is all.

Sexton And this is more, masters, than you can deny. Prince Don John is this morning secretly stolen away. Hero was in this manner accused, in this very manner refused, and upon the grief of this suddenly died. Master Constable, let these men be bound and brought to Leonato's. I will go before and show him their examination. *[Exit Sexton.]*

Dogberry Come, let them be opinioned.

Verges Let them be in the hands —

Conrade Off, coxcomb.

Dogberry God's my life, where's the Sexton? Let him write down "the Prince's officer coxcomb". Come, bind them. Thou naughty varlet!

Conrade Away! You are an ass, you are an ass.

Dogberry Dost thou not suspect my place? Dost thou not suspect my years? O that he were here to write me down an ass! But masters, remember that I am an ass. Though it be not written down, yet forget not that I am an ass. No, thou villain, thou art full of piety as shall be proved upon thee by good witness. I am a wise fellow, and which is more, an officer, and which is more, a householder, and which is more, as pretty a piece of flesh as any is in Messina. And one that knows the law, go to, and a rich fellow enough, go to, and a fellow that hath had losses, and one that hath two gowns, and everything handsome about him. Bring him away. O that I had been writ down an ass!

43 **Flat burglary:** downright burglary; he means villainy

50 **redemption:** salvation; he means the opposite: 'damnation'

60 **opinioned:** he means 'pinioned': tied up
62 **coxcomb:** fool
65 **naughty varlet:** wicked rogue
67 **suspect:** he means 'respect'
71 **piety:** respect for God; he means the opposite: 'impiety'
74 **householder:** a middle class man
74–5 **as pretty a piece of flesh:** as good-looking
76 **go to:** two meanings: hurry up; so there
77 **hath had losses:** has lost money
77 **hath two gowns:** again, suggests wealth; clothes were expensive

Director's Note, 4.2

- ✔ Dogberry fails to question Borachio, but the Sexton gets the evidence against Borachio and Conrade from the Watch.
- ✔ The Sexton ties up this story with what happened at the wedding, and tells Borachio and Conrade that Don John has fled, and Hero died.
- ✔ The Sexton orders Dogberry to take Borachio and Conrade to Leonato's house.

ACT 5 SCENE 1

Enter Leonato and his brother, Antonio.

Antonio
If you go on thus, you will kill yourself,
And 'tis not wisdom thus to second grief
Against yourself.

Leonato
I pray thee cease thy counsel,
Which falls into mine ears as profitless
As water in a sieve. Give not me counsel,
Nor let no comforter delight mine ear
But such a one whose wrongs do suit with mine.
Bring me a father that so loved his child,
Whose joy of her is overwhelmed like mine,
And bid him speak to me of patience.
Measure his woe the length and breadth of mine,
And let it answer every strain for strain,
As thus for thus, and such a grief for such,
In every lineament, branch, shape, and form.
If such a one will smile and stroke his beard,
And sorrow, wag, cry "hem" when he should groan,
Patch grief with proverbs, make misfortune drunk
With candle-wasters. Bring him yet to me,
And I of him will gather patience.
But there is no such man, for brother, men
Can counsel and speak comfort to that grief
Which they themselves not feel. But tasting it,
Their counsel turns to passion, which before
Would give preceptial medicine to rage,
Fetter strong madness in a silken thread,
Charm ache with air and agony with words.
No, no, 'tis all men's office to speak patience
To those that wring under the load of sorrow.
But no man's virtue nor sufficiency
To be so moral when he shall endure
The like himself. Therefore give me no counsel,
My griefs cry louder than advertisement.

Antonio
Therein do men from children nothing differ.

Leonato
I pray thee peace. I will be flesh and blood,
For there was never yet philosopher
That could endure the toothache patiently,
However they have writ the style of gods
And made a push at chance and sufferance.

Antonio
Yet bend not all the harm upon yourself,
Make those that do offend you suffer too.

Leonato
There thou speak'st reason. Nay, I will do so.
My soul doth tell me Hero is belied,
And that shall Claudio know, so shall the Prince,
And all of them that thus dishonour her.

Enter Don Pedro and Claudio.

2 **second:** take the side of
3 **counsel:** advice
4 **as profitless:** as uselessly
7 **do suit with:** match
12 **answer every strain for strain:** two meanings: 1) reflect my grief; 2) play back the same tune
14 **lineament:** outline
16 **wag:** shake his head
17 **Patch:** try to mend
18 **candle-wasters:** people who stay up late at night, studying
22 **not feel:** do not feel
23–4 **which before … medicine to rage:** who previously preached sermons against anger
25 **Fetter:** handcuff
26 **Charm ache with air:** cure aches with talking
27 **'tis all men's office:** everyone sees it as their job
28 **wring:** writhe in agony
28 **load:** weight
29–31 **no man's virtue or sufficiency … The like himself:** no one can preach patience to themselves when they suffer in the same way
32 **advertisement:** the advice of others
34 **I pray thee peace:** please be quiet
37 **writ the style of gods:** written claiming to be all-knowing gods
38 **made a push at:** dismissed
38 **sufferance:** suffering

Antonio Here comes the Prince and Claudio hastily.

Don Pedro Good e'en, good e'en.

Claudio Good day to both of you.

Leonato Hear you my lords?

Don Pedro We have some haste Leonato.

Leonato Some haste, my lord! Well, fare you well, my lord.
Are you so hasty now? Well, all is one.

Don Pedro Nay, do not quarrel with us, good old man.

Antonio If he could right himself with quarrelling,
Some of us would lie low.

Claudio Who wrongs him?

Leonato Marry thou dost wrong me, thou dissembler, thou!
Nay, never lay thy hand upon thy sword,
I fear thee not.

Claudio Marry beshrew my hand
If it should give your age such cause of fear.
In faith, my hand meant nothing to my sword.

46 **e'en:** any time after noon
47 **Hear you:** will you stop and listen to me?
47 **We have some haste:** we're in a hurry
49 **all is one:** it makes no difference
53 **thou dissembler:** you liar
54 **never lay thy hand upon thy sword:** don't dare touch your sword
55 **beshrew:** curse
56 **If it should give ... cause for fear:** if it made an old man think it might fight him
57 **my hand meant nothing to my sword:** I had no intention of challenging you

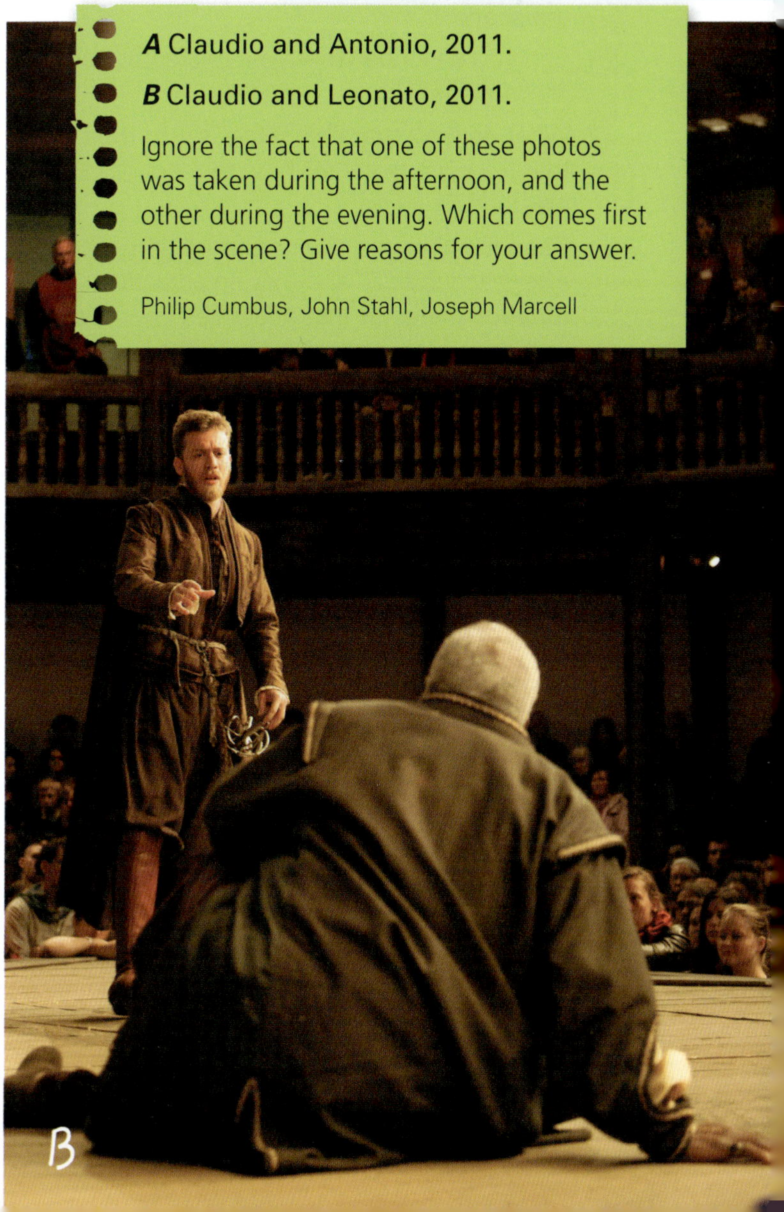

A Claudio and Antonio, 2011.

B Claudio and Leonato, 2011.

Ignore the fact that one of these photos was taken during the afternoon, and the other during the evening. Which comes first in the scene? Give reasons for your answer.

Philip Cumbus, John Stahl, Joseph Marcell

FROM THE REHEARSAL ROOM...

SHAKESPEARE AS DIRECTOR

In groups of four, read the *Working Cut* of Act 5 Scene 1.

- Decide who will read each part. They are: Leonato, Don Pedro, Claudio and Antonio. Sit facing each other.
- Read through the *Working Cut* and each time your character is given a stage direction or makes a movement in the text, repeat the word or phrase.
- Now, read the *Working Cut* again, and this time repeat the words or phrases that describe how your character is feeling or what they are thinking.
- Read the *Working Cut* again and this time repeat the words and phrases that the other characters say about what you do, how you react and how you express your feelings in the scene.

1 Can you describe what your character has to do on stage?

2 What do the other characters say in their lines that tell your character how to react or move on stage?

- Read the *Working Cut* one more time. Stop after each speech and pick an adjective for your character that describes how your character feels at each point in the scene.
- Look carefully at the sequence of adjectives. These words reveal your character's emotional journey in the scene. What do you notice about their state of mind in this scene?
- Compare your character's emotional journey with those of the other three characters in the scene. Discuss what you notice about their state of mind.

3 Are the characters' emotional journeys similar or different?

Working Cut – text for experiment

Antonio Here comes the Prince and Claudio hastily.
Don Pedro Good e'en, good e'en.
Leonato Hear you my lords?
Don Pedro We have some haste Leonato.
Leonato Are you so hasty now? Well, all is one.
Don Pedro Nay, do not quarrel with us, good old man.
Claudio Who wrongs him?
Leonato Marry thou dost wrong me, thou dissembler, thou!
Nay, never lay thy hand upon thy sword,
I fear thee not.
Claudio Marry beshrew my hand
If it should give your age such cause of fear.
In faith, my hand meant nothing to my sword.
Leonato Tush, tush, man, never fleer and jest at me.
Thou hast so wronged mine innocent child and me
That I am forced to lay my reverence by,
And with grey hairs and bruise of many days,
Do challenge thee to trial of a man.
I say thou hast belied mine innocent child.
Thy slander hath gone through and through her heart,
And she lied buried with her ancestors.
O, in a tomb where never scandal slept,
Save this of hers, framed by thy villainy.
Claudio My villainy?
Leonato Thine Claudio, thine I say.
Don Pedro You say not right, old man.
Leonato My lord, my lord,
I'll prove it on his body if he dare,
Despite his nice fence, and his active practice,
His May of youth and bloom of lustihood.
Claudio Away! I will not have to do with you.
Leonato Canst thou so daff me? Thou hast killed my child,
If thou kill'st me, boy, thou shalt kill a man.
Antonio He shall kill two of us, and men indeed
Come follow me boy, come sir boy, come follow me
Leonato Brother –
Antonio Content yourself. God knows I loved my niece,
And she is dead, slandered to death by villains,
That dare as well answer a man indeed
As I dare take a serpent by the tongue.
Boys, apes, braggarts, jacks, milksops.
Leonato But brother Anthony –
Antonio Come, 'tis no matter.
Do not you meddle, let me deal in this.
Don Pedro Gentlemen both, we will not wake your patience,
My heart is sorry for your daughter's death.
But on my honour she was charged with nothing
But what was true, and very full of proof.
Leonato My lord, my lord–
Don Pedro I will not hear you.
Leonato No.
Come brother, away, I will be heard.
Antonio And shall, or some of us will smart for it.
[Exit Leonato and Antonio.]

Leonato Tush, tush, man, never fleer and jest at me.
I speak not like a dotard nor a fool,
As under privilege of age to brag
What I have done being young, or what would do
Were I not old. Know, Claudio, to thy head,
Thou hast so wronged mine innocent child and me
That I am forced to lay my reverence by,
And with grey hairs and bruise of many days,
Do challenge thee to trial of a man.
I say thou hast belied mine innocent child.
Thy slander hath gone through and through her heart,
And she lied buried with her ancestors.
O, in a tomb where never scandal slept,
Save this of hers, framed by thy villainy.

Claudio My villainy?

Leonato Thine Claudio, thine I say.

Don Pedro You say not right, old man.

Leonato My lord, my lord,
I'll prove it on his body if he dare,
Despite his nice fence, and his active practice,
His May of youth and bloom of lustihood.

Claudio Away! I will not have to do with you.

Leonato Canst thou so daff me? Thou hast killed my child,
If thou kill'st me, boy, thou shalt kill a man.

Antonio He shall kill two of us, and men indeed,
But that's no matter, let him kill one first.
Win me and wear me, let him answer me.
Come follow me boy, come sir boy, come follow me
Sir boy. I'll whip you from your foining fence.
Nay, as I am a gentleman, I will.

Leonato Brother —

Antonio Content yourself. God knows I loved my niece,
And she is dead, slandered to death by villains,
That dare as well answer a man indeed
As I dare take a serpent by the tongue.
Boys, apes, braggarts, jacks, milksops.

Leonato Brother Anthony —

Antonio Hold you content. What, man? I know them, yea
And what they weigh, even to the utmost scruple.
Scambling, outfacing, fashion-monging boys,
That lie, and cog, and flout, deprave and slander,
Go anticly, and show outward hideousness,
And speak off half a dozen dang'rous words,
How they might hurt their enemies, if they durst.
And this is all.

Leonato But brother Anthony —

Antonio Come, 'tis no matter.
Do not you meddle, let me deal in this.

58 **fleer:** mock
59 **dotard:** senile old man
60–62 **As under privilege of age ... Were I not old:** taking refuge in my age to boast of past fights and how I would fight if only I was young
62 **to thy head:** I say this to your face
64 **lay my reverence by:** put aside my age
65 **bruise of many days:** wear and tear of years
66 **trial of a man:** a duel
70 **never scandal slept:** noone buried there has ever been involved in scandal
71 **framed:** fabricated, made up
74 **on his body:** by killing him
75 **nice fence:** skill with a sword
75 **active practice:** regular training
76 **May of youth and bloom of lustihood:** youthful energy
78 **daff me:** brush me aside
82 **Win me and wear me:** he has to beat me to boast of it
82 **answer me:** accept my challenge
84 **foining fence:** showy swordplay
89–90 **That dare as well ... by the tongue:** who doesn't dare duel with a real man, any more than I'd pick up a snake by the tongue
92 **Hold you content:** Hush
93 **weigh:** are worth
93 **utmost scruple:** last little bit
94 **Scambling, outfacing, fashion-monging:** quarrelsome, shameless, vain
95 **cog:** cheat
95 **flout:** mock
95 **deprave:** ruin
96 **Go anticly:** dress appallingly
96 **show outward hideousness:** act scary
98 **durst:** chose
101 **deal in this:** sort this out

Actor's view

Philip Cumbus
Claudio, 2011

Claudio's relationship with Benedick starts out as very [close]. He's the first person that Claudio goes to, to say 'I'm having these very strange feelings about this girl and I don't quite know what they mean', because he has a connection with Benedick. But then later on that relationship starts to sort of sour a little bit. It gets a bit more arched, because of the challenge and the potential duel that they're going to have. It leaves a bitterness between them and the banter starts to take on a more dark, aggressive tone towards the end of the play. And whether Claudio and Benedick will ever again have that sort of relationship is, I think, quite unclear. It might forever be tainted by the events that have happened in the play.

Claudio is a good man to hang around with in battle because he's an incredibly effective soldier. So the duel is quite funny, I think, if you make it that the duel has a very clear outcome – that Claudio would obviously be victorious. It means also for Benedick it's a bigger deal for him if he says 'I challenge you', because he knows that it would be a very tough fight.

SHAKESPEARE'S WORLD

Duels and men's ideas of honour

In Shakespeare's world, a man's reputation was very important. Men, especially upper class men, would fight to preserve their honour. In this scene Benedick challenges Claudio to a duel – a fight to the death with swords. Benedick has promised Beatrice to challenge Claudio to defend Hero's reputation, even though Claudio is his friend. 'I am engaged,' he says, 'I will challenge him' (Act 4 Scene 1 line 324). 'Engaged' means committed to fight. Benedick cannot change his mind about fighting for Hero's honour without losing his own.

Benedick points out that Claudio's honour is at stake too. 'Do me right, or I will protest your cowardice', he says to Claudio (Act 5 Scene 1 line 142). If Claudio refuses the challenge, he will be dishonoured, and called a coward. Honourable men were not cowards. Shakespeare's audience would have been familiar with the idea of duelling and what is at stake in this scene. All gentlemen at the time carried swords. Duelling was against the law. However, the idea that a duel would settle an argument where a man's honour was a stake was still so strong that duels were often fought.

Claudio and Benedick, 2011.

Was this photo taken during line 118, line 138, or between lines 140 and 144? Give reasons for your answer.

Philip Cumbus, Charles Edwards

Don Pedro Gentlemen both, we will not wake your patience,
My heart is sorry for your daughter's death.
But on my honour she was charged with nothing
But what was true, and very full of proof.

Leonato My lord, my lord —

Don Pedro I will not hear you.

Leonato No.
Come brother, away, I will be heard.

Antonio And shall, or some of us will smart for it.

Exit Leonato and Antonio. Enter Benedick.

Don Pedro See, see! Here comes the man we went to seek.

Claudio Now, signor, what news?

Benedick *[To Don Pedro.]* Good day my lord.

Don Pedro Welcome signor. You are almost come to part almost a fray.

Claudio We had liked to have had our two noses snapped off with two old men without teeth.

Don Pedro Leonato and his brother. What think'st thou? Had we fought, I doubt we should have been too young for them.

Benedick In a false quarrel there is no true valour. I came to seek you both.

Claudio We have been up and down to seek thee, for we are high-proof melancholy, and would fain have it beaten away. Wilt thou use thy wit?

Benedick It is in my scabbard, shall I draw it?

Don Pedro Dost thou wear thy wit by thy side?

Claudio Never any did so, though very many have been beside their wit. I will bid thee draw, as we do the minstrels, draw to pleasure us.

Don Pedro As I am an honest man, he looks pale. Art thou sick, or angry?

Claudio What, courage man. What though care killed a cat, thou hast mettle enough in thee to kill care.

Benedick Sir, I shall meet your wit in the career an you charge it against me. I pray you choose another subject.

Claudio Nay then, give him another staff, this last was broke cross.

Don Pedro *[To Claudio.]* By this light, he changes more and more.
I think he be angry indeed.

Claudio *[To Don Pedro.]* If he be, he knows how to turn his girdle.

Benedick Shall I speak a word in your ear?

Claudio God bless me from a challenge.

102 **wake your patience:** annoy you any longer
108 **smart:** suffer
112–3 **You are almost come to part almost a fray:** you nearly had to break up a fight
114 **had liked to have:** nearly had
115 **with:** by
117 **I doubt:** I fear
121 **high-proof:** extremely
121 **would fain have it:** want it
125–6 **beside their wit:** out of their minds
127 **draw to pleasure us:** draw your bow over a musical instrument's stings, to please us
130 **care killed a cat:** a proverb meaning worrying is bad for you
131 **mettle:** courage
132 **in the career:** at full gallop (this starts a run of puns on jousting)
132 **an you:** if you
134 **staff:** refers to a jousting pole
134 **broke cross:** broken hitting his opponent sideways, not point first (only a bad jouster would do this)
135 **By this light, he changes more and more:** I'll swear he's more and more different
137 **turn his girdle:** put up with it
139 **God bless me:** God save me from

build stage society at beginning of the play Act IV Scene 1

Benedick and Claudio, 2008.

Compare this photo with the one on page 98. Was this photo taken during line 118, line 138, or between lines 140 and 144? Give reasons for your answer.

Bill Buckhurst, Navin Chowdhry

FROM THE REHEARSAL ROOM...

CONFRONTATIONS

In groups of six, decide on three people to read each part. They are: Don Pedro, Claudio and Benedick. The rest will be 'listeners' – one for each character.

- As you read through the extract, the 'listeners' should repeat any words or phrases that are powerful, reveal information or tell us how their character is feeling in the scene.

1. Note or highlight all the words or phrases that were repeated.
2. Collect all the words from the group and organise them into three lists, one for each character: Don Pedro, Claudio and Benedick.
3. What do the lists of words tell us about Benedick's goal in this extract?
4. How do Don Pedro and Claudio respond to Benedick's confrontation? Support your opinions with quotes from the text.
5. Describe how this challenge is similar or different to other confrontations in the play.
6. What does the extract tell us about Benedick's character? Quote from the text to support your answer.

Working Cut – text for experiment

Don Pedro Welcome signor. You are almost come to part almost a fray.

Claudio We had liked to have had our two noses snapped off with two old men without teeth.

Don Pedro Leonato and his brother. What think'st thou? Had we fought, I doubt we should have been too young for them.

Benedick In a false quarrel there is no true valour. I came to seek you both.

Claudio We have been up and down to seek thee, for we are high-proof melancholy, and would fain have it beaten away. Wilt thou use thy wit?

Benedick It is in my scabbard, shall I draw it?

Claudio I will bid thee draw, as we do the minstrels, draw to pleasure us.

Don Pedro As I am an honest man, he looks pale. Art thou sick, or angry?

Claudio What, courage man. What though care killed a cat, thou hast mettle enough in thee to kill care.

Benedick Sir, I shall meet your wit in the career an you charge it against me. I pray you choose another subject.

Don Pedro *[To Claudio.]* By this light, he changes more and more. I think he be angry indeed.

Benedick Shall I speak a word in your ear?

Claudio God bless me from a challenge.

Benedick *[To Claudio.]* You are a villain. I jest not, I will make it good how you dare, with what you dare, and when you dare. Do me right, or I will protest your cowardice. You have killed a sweet lady, and her death shall fall heavy on you. Let me hear from you.

Claudio Well I will meet you so I will have good cheer

Don Pedro What a feast, a feast?

Benedick Fare you well, boy, you know my mind. I will leave you now to your gossip-like humour. My lord, for your many courtesies I thank you. I must discontinue your company. Your brother the Bastard is fled from Messina. You have among you killed a sweet and innocent lady. For my Lord Lackbeard there, he and I shall meet, and till then peace be with him.
[Exit Benedick.]

Benedick *[To Claudio.]* You are a villain. I jest not, I will make it good how you dare, with what you dare, and when you dare. Do me right, or I will protest your cowardice. You have killed a sweet lady, and her death shall fall heavy on you. Let me hear from you.

Claudio Well, I will meet you, so I may have good cheer.

Don Pedro What, a feast, a feast?

Claudio I'faith I thank him. He hath bid me to a calf's head and a capon, the which if I do not carve most curiously, say my knife's naught. Shall I not find a woodcock too?

Benedick Sir, your wit ambles well, it goes easily.

Don Pedro I'll tell thee how Beatrice praised thy wit the other day. I said thou hadst a fine wit. "True," said she, "a fine little one." "No," said I, "a great wit." "Right," says she, "a great gross one." "Nay," said I, "a good wit." "Just," said she, "it hurts nobody." "Nay," said I, "the gentleman is wise." "Certain," said she, "a wise gentleman." "Nay," said I, "he hath the tongues." "That I believe," said she, "for he swore a thing to me on Monday night which he forswore on Tuesday morning. There's a double tongue, there's two tongues." Thus did she an hour together trans-shape thy particular virtues. Yet at last she concluded with a sigh, thou wast the properest man in Italy.

Claudio For the which she wept heartily and said she cared not.

Don Pedro Yea, that she did, but yet, for all that, and if she did not hate him deadly, she would love him dearly. The old man's daughter told us all.

Claudio All, all. And moreover, God saw him when he was hid in the garden.

Don Pedro But when shall we set the savage bull's horns on the sensible Benedick's head?

Claudio Yea, and text underneath, "Here dwells Benedick, the married man".

Benedick Fare you well, boy, you know my mind. I will leave you now to your gossip-like humour. You break jests as braggards do their blades, which God be thanked hurt not. My lord, for your many courtesies I thank you. I must discontinue your company. Your brother the Bastard is fled from Messina. You have among you killed a sweet and innocent lady. For my Lord Lackbeard there, he and I shall meet, and till then peace be with him. *[Exit Benedick.]*

Don Pedro He is in earnest.

Claudio In most profound earnest, and, I'll warrant you, for the love of Beatrice.

140–1 **make it good:** show I mean what I say (by fighting a duel)
141–2 **how you dare ... when you dare:** challenges Claudio to choose the time, place and weapons for the duel
142 **Do me right:** accept my challenge
142 **protest:** publicly announce
145 **meet you:** accept your challenge
145 **cheer:** entertainment
147–9 **calf's head/capon/woodcock:** foods that are also insults: fool/ cuckold whose wife has been unfaithful to him/idiot
148 **carve most curiously:** double meaning: carving food; cutting with his sword
150 **goes easily:** is slow
155 **Just:** exactly so
157 **hath the tongues:** speaks several languages
159 **forswore:** took back as seriously
161 **trans-shape:** distort
163 **properest:** most handsome
170 **savage bull's horns:** a cuckold is said to have horns when his wife is unfaithful
175 **your gossip-like humour:** get on with your trivial chatter
176 **as braggards do their blades:** in the same way boastful men damage their swords to pretend they've been fighting
180–1 **my Lord Lackbeard:** referring to Claudio's youth – boy
184 **I'll warrant you:** I assure you

George Seacole, Conrade, Don Pedro, Borachio (kneeling), Dogberry, Verges and Claudio, 2011.

After Dogberry and his prisoners enter there are two very different moods in the text on page 103. First, it is humorous, as Don Pedro mocks Dogberry, then it turns serious. Was this photo taken during the humorous or the serious section? Give reasons for your answer.

David Nellist, Marcus Griffiths, Ewan Stewart, Joe Caffrey, Paul Hunter, Adrian Hood, Philip Cumbus

FROM THE REHEARSAL ROOM...

BORACHIO'S STORY – FRAMING THE ACTION

- Divide into groups of five.
- Read through Borachio's description of the recent events surrounding Hero's death (lines 213–225).
- Read the extract again, and this time identify the sequence of events.
- In your groups, create a freeze frame to illustrate each part of the story that Borachio tells.
- Next, using the text to inspire your choices, add a title to each freeze frame.
- Run each freeze frame in sequence with their titles.
- Compare each group's interpretation of Borachio's version of events.

1 What is the purpose of Borachio's story?
2 How do the different people in the scene react to his confession?
3 What is the impact of his story on Claudio?

Don Pedro And hath challenged thee?

Claudio Most sincerely.

Don Pedro What a pretty thing man is, when he goes in his doublet and hose, and leaves off his wit.

Claudio He is then a giant to an ape, but then is an ape a doctor to such a man.

Don Pedro But, soft you, let me be, pluck up my heart, and be sad. Did he not say my brother was fled?

Enter Dogberry and Verges, with the Watch, leading Conrade and Borachio as prisoners.

Dogberry Come you sir, if justice cannot tame you, she shall ne'er weigh more reasons in her balance. Nay, an you be a cursing hypocrite once, you must be looked to.

Don Pedro How now, two of my brother's men bound? Borachio one.

Claudio Hearken after their offence my lord.

Don Pedro Officers, what offence have these men done?

Dogberry Marry sir, they have committed false report. Moreover, they have spoken untruths. Secondarily, they are slanders. Sixth and lastly, they have belied a lady. Thirdly, they have verified unjust things. And to conclude they are lying knaves.

Don Pedro First, I ask thee what they have done? Thirdly I ask thee what's their offence? Sixth and lastly, why they are committed. And to conclude, what you lay to their charge?

Claudio Rightly reasoned, and in his own division, and by my troth there's one meaning well suited.

Don Pedro Who have you offended masters, that you are thus bound to your answer? This learnèd Constable is too cunning to be understood. What's your offence?

Borachio Sweet Prince, let me go no farther to mine answer. Do you hear me, and let this Count kill me. I have deceived even your very eyes. What your wisdoms could not discover, these shallow fools have brought to light, who in the night overheard me confessing to this man how Don John your brother incensed me to slander the Lady Hero, how you were brought into the orchard and saw me court Margaret in Hero's garments, how you disgraced her when you should marry her. My villainy they have upon record, which I had rather seal with my death than repeat over to my shame. The lady is dead upon mine and my master's false accusation. And briefly, I desire nothing but the reward of a villain.

Don Pedro *[To Claudio.]* Runs not this speech like iron through your blood?

Claudio *[To Don Pedro.]* I have drunk poison whiles he uttered it.

188 **pretty:** said ironically to mean 'awkward'
188 **goes in:** goes out in
189 **leaves off his wit:** doesn't take his intelligence
190–1 **He is then a giant ... to such a man:** he seems clever to an idiot, but really the idiot is far wiser than he is
192 **soft you, let me be ... and be sad:** wait, give me a moment to think seriously
194–5 **ne'er weigh more reasons in her balance:** never again weigh evidence in her scales
196 **looked to:** punished
198 **Hearken after their offence:** ask what crime they have committed
202 **slanders:** he means 'slanderers'
203 **verified:** he means 'testified'
208 **Rightly reasoned:** well argued
208 **in his own division:** as badly classified as his
211 **bound to your answer:** a pun; both tied up and compelled to face charges
212 **cunning:** clever
213 **go no farther to mine answer:** tell you straight away
215 **your wisdoms:** you clever men
218 **incensed:** urged
222 **upon record:** written down
223 **repeat over:** repeat
224 **upon:** because of
226–7 **Runs not this speech ... through your blood?:** doesn't this make your blood run cold?

Leonato, Don Pedro, Claudio, the Watch, prisoners kneeling and Antonio (standing to the side), 2011.

This photo was taken during one of Leonato's speeches – which one? Give reasons for your answer.

Joseph Marcell, Ewan Stewart, Philip Cumbus, John Stahl

Don Pedro *[To Borachio.]* But did my brother set thee on to this?

Borachio Yea, and paid me richly for the practice of it.

Don Pedro He is composed and framed of treachery,
And fled he is upon this villainy.

Claudio Sweet Hero, now thy image doth appear
In the rare semblance that I loved it first.

Dogberry Come, bring away the plaintiffs. By this time our sexton hath reformed Signor Leonato of the matter. And masters, do not forget to specify when time and place shall serve, that I am an ass.

Verges Here, here comes Master Signor Leonato, and the sexton too.

Enter Leonato, his brother, Antonio, and the sexton.

Leonato Which is the villain? Let me see his eyes,
That when I note another man like him,
I may avoid him. Which of these is he?

Borachio If you would know your wronger, look on me.

Leonato Art thou the slave that with thy breath hast killed
Mine innocent child?

Borachio Yea, even I alone.

Leonato No, not so villain, thou beliest thyself.
Here stand a pair of honourable men,
A third is fled that had a hand in it.
I thank you, Princes, for my daughter's death.
Record it with your high and worthy deeds,
'Twas bravely done, if you bethink you of it.

Claudio I know not how to pray your patience,
Yet I must speak. Choose your revenge yourself,
Impose me to what penance your invention
Can lay upon my sin. Yet sinned I not
But in mistaking.

Don Pedro By my soul, nor I.
And yet to satisfy this good old man,
I would bend under any heavy weight
That he'll enjoin me to.

Leonato I cannot bid you bid my daughter live,
That were impossible, but I pray you both,
Possess the people in Messina here
How innocent she died. *[To Claudio.]* And if your love
Can labour aught in sad invention,
Hang her an epitaph upon her tomb,
And sing it to her bones. Sing it tonight.
Tomorrow morning come you to my house,
And since you could not be my son-in-law,
Be yet my nephew. My brother hath a daughter,
Almost the copy of my child that's dead,
And she alone is heir to both of us.

230 **the practice of it:** doing it
231 **composed and framed of:** made up of
232 **upon this villainy:** having done this wicked thing
234 **rare semblance:** exceptional appearance
235 **the plaintiffs:** people who accuse someone of a crime; he means 'accused'
236 **reformed:** he means 'informed'
245 **slave:** used as an insult
245 **with thy breath:** by your words
248 **honourable men:** said ironically of Don Pedro and Claudio, blaming them too
249 **A third:** Don John
253 **pray:** beg
255–6 **Impose me to what penance your invention Can lay upon my sin:** punish me in whatever way you want
256–7 **sinned I not But in mistaking:** it was an honest mistake
259–60 **weight That he'll enjoin me to:** punishment he'll give me
263 **Possess:** tell
265 **labour aught in sad invention:** is able to compose serious poetry
266 **epitaph:** verse praising a dead person

Dogberry

A 2004, *B* 2011, *C* 2008.

1 Dogberry is one of Shakespeare's comic characters, who would have been played by the clown in his company. Have the director, designer and actors made Dogberry look a comic character in these three productions? Explain your answer.

2 Which version of Dogberry's costume and body language do you think is the most successful? Give reasons for your answer.

A Sarah Woodward; ***B*** Paul Hunter; ***C*** Tony Taylor

Actor's view

Paul Hunter
Dogberry, 2011

[The Watch] is a group of men who, in some ways, have responsibility but they're slightly ridiculous and ludicrous at trying to be this authority which they can't really do.

The gap between how Dogberry sees himself and how the world sees him is quite enormous and I think that's rather good for comedy. He sees himself, I'm sure, as a very good policeman and a very important man whereas actually the world sees him as a rather ridiculous man and that's always great.

Give her the right you should have giv'n her cousin,
And so dies my revenge.

Claudio O noble sir!
Your over-kindness doth wring tears from me.
I do embrace your offer, and dispose
For henceforth of poor Claudio.

Leonato Tomorrow then I will expect your coming,
Tonight I take my leave. This naughty man
Shall face to face be brought to Margaret,
Who I believe was packed in all this wrong,
Hired to it by your brother.

Borachio No, by my soul, she was not,
Nor knew not what she did when she spoke to me,
But always hath been just and virtuous
In anything that I do know by her.

Dogberry Moreover sir, which indeed is not under white and black, this plaintiff here, the offender, did call me ass. I beseech you let it be remembered in his punishment. And also the Watch heard them talk of one Deformed. They say he wears a key in his ear and a lock hanging by it, and borrows money in God's name, the which he hath used so long and never paid, that now men grow hard-hearted and will lend nothing for God's sake. Pray you examine him upon that point.

Leonato I thank thee for thy care and honest pains.

Dogberry Your worship speaks like a most thankful and reverent youth, and I praise God for you.

Leonato *[Giving money.]* There's for thy pains.

Dogberry God save the foundation!

Leonato Go, I discharge thee of thy prisoner, and I thank thee.

Dogberry I leave an arrant knave with your worship, which I beseech your worship to correct yourself, for the example of others. God keep your worship! I wish your worship well! God restore you to health! I humbly give you leave to depart, and if a merry meeting may be wished, God prohibit it! Come neighbour.

Exit Dogberry and Verges.

Leonato Until tomorrow morning, lords, farewell.

Antonio Farewell, my lords, we look for you tomorrow.

Don Pedro We will not fail.

Claudio Tonight I'll mourn with Hero.

Leonato *[To the Watch.]* Bring you these fellows on. – We'll talk with Margaret, how her acquaintance grew with this lewd fellow.

They all exit.

273 **Give her the right:** marry her
276–7 **dispose For henceforth of poor Claudio:** give you control of worthless Claudio
279 **naughty:** wicked
281 **packed:** tangled up in
286 **by:** of
287–8 **under white and black:** he means 'in black and white': written down
288 **plaintiff:** the accuser; he means 'accused'
292 **borrows money in God's name:** begs
296 **thy care and honest pains:** the trouble you've taken
297 **thankful:** he means 'generous'
297 **reverent:** old and respected
298 **praise:** he means 'thank'
300 **God save the foundation:** the phrase a beggar used when given money by a charitable group
305–6 **give you leave to depart:** you can go: he means 'ask your permission to depart'
307 **prohibit it:** stop it: he means 'make it happen'
309 **look for you:** will expect you
314 **lewd:** used here to mean wicked

Director's Note, 5.1

- ✔ Leonato and Antonio both challenge Claudio, but he does not take them seriously.
- ✔ Benedick arrives, and he challenges Claudio to a duel, which he accepts.
- ✔ The Watch bring in Borachio and Conrade. Borachio confesses to what he has done.
- ✔ Leonato and Antonio return, having been told by the Sexton. Claudio asks for Leonato's forgiveness, and is told he must commemorate Hero, then marry Leonato's niece.
- ✔ Are all the misunderstandings now cleared up?

Benedick: *A* 2011, *B* 2008.

1. Who is the actor in Photo A making eye contact with? Why do you think he is doing this?
2. Which of the photographs comes from earlier in the scene? Quote from the text to support your answer.

A Charles Edwards; ***B*** Bill Buckhurst

ACT 5 SCENE 2

Enter Benedick and Margaret.

Benedick Pray thee, sweet Mistress Margaret, deserve well at my hands by helping me to the speech of Beatrice.

Margaret Will you then write me a sonnet in praise of my beauty?

Benedick In so high a style, Margaret, that no man living shall come over it, for in most comely truth thou deservest it.

Margaret To have no man come over me? Why, shall I always keep below stairs?

Benedick Thy wit is as quick as the greyhound's mouth, it catches.

Margaret And yours as blunt as the fencer's foils, which hit but hurt not.

Benedick A most manly wit Margaret, it will not hurt a woman. And so I pray thee call Beatrice. I give thee the bucklers.

Margaret Give us the swords, we have bucklers of our own.

Benedick If you use them, Margaret, you must put in the pikes with a vice, and they are dangerous weapons for maids.

Margaret Well, I will call Beatrice to you, who I think hath legs.

Exit Margaret.

Benedick And therefore will come.

[Sings.]

The god of love
That sits above,
And knows me, and knows me,
How pitiful I deserve —

I mean in singing. But in loving, Leander the good swimmer, Troilus the first employer of panders, and a whole book full of these quondam carpet-mongers, whose names yet run smoothly in the even road of a blank verse — why, they were never so truly turned over and over as my poor self in love. Marry, I cannot show it in rhyme. I have tried. I can find out no rhyme to "lady" but "baby," an innocent rhyme, for "scorn," "horn," a hard rhyme, for "school," "fool," a babbling rhyme. Very ominous endings. No, I was not born under a rhyming planet, nor I cannot woo in festival terms.

Enter Beatrice.

Sweet Beatrice, wouldst thou come when I called thee?

Beatrice Yea signor, and depart when you bid me.

Benedick O stay but till then.

Beatrice "Then" is spoken, fare you well now. And yet, ere I go, let me go with that I came for, which is, with knowing what hath passed between you and Claudio.

Benedick Only foul words, and thereupon I will kiss thee.

Beatrice Foul words is but foul wind, and foul wind is but foul

---

1–2 **deserve well at my hands:** earn my gratitude
2 **to the speech of:** to get to talk to
4 **In so high a style:** double meaning: 1) so beautifully written; 2) such a high 'stile' to cross a fence
5 **come over it:** double meaning: 1) write anything better; 2) climb the stile
5 **comely:** pleasing to look at (punning on both 'come over' and 'plain truth')
6 **To have no man come over me:** she moves the puns into sexual double meanings
7 **keep below stairs:** remain a servant
8 **Thy wit is ... it catches:** you're quick to notice a pun and play the game
9 **foils:** light swords for fencing, not real fighting
12 **I give thee the bucklers:** I surrender (bucklers were small round shields)
13 **swords:** used here with a sexual double meaning and punned on until she leaves
21 ***pitiful I deserve*:** unworthy I am
22 **Leander:** a lover in Greek legend
23 **Troilus:** a lover in medieval legends of the siege of Troy
23 **panders:** someone who helps lovers to meet
24–6 **quondam carpet-mongers ... blank verse:** ladies men of the past who have had poems written about them
31–2 **I was not born ... planet:** people at the time believed the position of stars and planets when you were born affected your character
32 **festival terms:** poetic language
36 **ere:** before
37 **let me go with:** I must have
37 **with knowing:** to know
40–1 **Foul words is but foul wind ... noisome:** harsh words are nothing but hot air, which is nothing but bad breath, which smells disgusting

A

Benedick and Beatrice, 2011.

Study the text from Beatrice's entrance (page 109) to her exit.

1 Which of these two photos was taken first? Quote from the text to support your answer.

2 Pick a line or phrase to be a caption for each photo, and explain the reasons for your choice.

Charles Edwards, Eve Best

B

breath, and foul breath is noisome, therefore I will depart unkissed.

Benedick Thou hast frighted the word out of his right sense, so forcible is thy wit. But I must tell thee plainly, Claudio undergoes my challenge, and either I must shortly hear from him or I will subscribe him a coward. And I pray thee now tell me, for which of my bad parts didst thou first fall in love with me?

Beatrice For them all together, which maintained so politic a state of evil that they will not admit any good part to intermingle with them. But for which of my good parts did you first suffer love for me?

Benedick Suffer love! A good epithet. I do suffer love indeed, for I love thee against my will.

Beatrice In spite of your heart, I think. Alas poor heart! If you spite it for my sake, I will spite it for yours, for I will never love that which my friend hates.

Benedick Thou and I are too wise to woo peaceably.

Beatrice It appears not in this confession. There's not one wise man among twenty that will praise himself.

Benedick An old, an old instance, Beatrice, that lived in the time of good neighbours. If a man do not erect in this age his own tomb ere he dies, he shall live no longer in monument than the bell rings and the widow weeps.

Beatrice And how long is that, think you?

Benedick Question, why an hour in clamour and a quarter in rheum. Therefore is it most expedient for the wise, if Don Worm (his conscience), find no impediment to the contrary, to be the trumpet of his own virtues, as I am to myself. So much for praising myself, who, I myself will bear witness is praiseworthy. And now tell me, how doth your cousin?

Beatrice Very ill.

Benedick And how do you?

Beatrice Very ill too.

Benedick Serve God, love me, and mend. *Enter Ursula.* There will I leave you too, for here comes one in haste.

Ursula Madam, you must come to your uncle, yonder's old coil at home, it is proved my Lady Hero hath been falsely accused, the Prince and Claudio mightily abused, and Don John is the author of all, who is fled and gone. Will you come presently?

Beatrice Will you go hear this news signor?

Benedick I will live in thy heart, die in thy lap, and be buried in thy eyes. And moreover, I will go with thee to thy uncle's.

They all exit.

45 **undergoes my challenge:** will fight me
45–6 **I must shortly hear from him:** he must soon tell me where, when and with what he wants to fight
46 **subscribe him:** publicly announce that he is
49–50 **maintained so politic a state of evil:** kept up such an evil front
53 **epithet:** choice of words
58 **too wise:** used here to mean 'too keen to show how clever we are'
59 **this confession:** what you've just said
61–2 **that lived in time of good neighbours:** that dates from the good old days
62–4 **If a man do not ... the widow weeps:** now you have to build your own tomb while you live, otherwise you won't be remembered long
66 **clamour:** the ringing of the funeral bell
67 **rheum:** the widow's tears
67 **is it most expedient:** the best plan
76 **mend:** be cured
78 **yonder's old coil:** all hell's broken loose
80 **abused:** deceived
82 **presently:** straight away
84 **die in thy lap:** a sexual reference, die was slang for orgasm
85 **moreover:** as well as all that

Director's Note, 5.2

- ✔ Benedick finds it hard to write a love poem about Beatrice.
- ✔ When she arrives he tells her he has challenged Claudio.
- ✔ Ursula tells them the plot has been discovered, and Don John is responsible.
- ✔ Are there any misunderstandings in this scene?

ACT 5 SCENE 3

Enter Claudio, Don Pedro, and three or four Lords with tapers.

Claudio Is this the monument of Leonato?

A Lord It is my lord. *[He reads.]*

Done to death by slanderous tongues
Was the Hero that here lies
Death, in guerdon of her wrongs,
Gives her fame which never dies.
So the life that died with shame
Lives in death with glorious fame.

Claudio *[Hangs up the Epitaph.]*

Hang thou there upon the tomb,
Praising her when I am dumb.
Now music sound, and sing your solemn hymn.

A Lord

Pardon goddess of the night,
Those that slew thy virgin knight,
For the which with songs of woe,
Round about her tomb they go.
Midnight, assist our moan,
Help us to sigh and groan,
Heavily, heavily.
Graves yawn and yield your dead,
Till death be uttered,
Heavily, heavily.

1 **monument:** family tomb

5 **in guerdon of:** in repayment for

12 ***goddess of the night*:** Diana, also goddess of the moon and of chastity

13 ***thy virgin knight*:** her follower, Hero

20 **uttered:** fully explained

Don Pedro and Claudio before Hero's tomb, 2008.

How have the director and designer reflected the modern world in their choices for this scene? Explain your answer.

Tom Davey, Navin Chowdhry

Claudio Now unto thy bones good night.
Yearly will I do this rite.

Don Pedro Good morrow masters, put your torches out.
The wolves have preyed, and look, the gentle day
Before the wheels of Phoebus, round about
Dapples the drowsy east with spots of grey.
Thanks to you all, and leave us. Fare you well.

Claudio Good morrow masters. Each his several way.

[Exit all but Don Pedro and Claudio.]

Don Pedro Come, let us hence, and put on other weeds,
And then to Leonato's we will go.

Claudio And Hymen now with luckier issue speeds,
Than this for whom we rendered up this woe.

They exit.

24 **Good morrow:** good morning
26 **Phoebus:** the sun god, who drove a chariot
30 **weeds:** clothes
32–3 **Hymen now with luckier issue ... this woe:** let's hope the god of marriage brings a better outcome than he did for her we have just mourned (Hero)

Director's Note, 5.3

✔ Claudio and Don Pedro mourn Hero at her tomb. They both believe she is dead.

ACT 5 SCENE 4

Enter Leonato, Benedick, Beatrice, Margaret, Ursula, Antonio, Friar Francis and Hero.

Friar Did I not tell you she was innocent?

Leonato So are the Prince and Claudio, who accused her
Upon the error that you heard debated.
But Margaret was in some fault for this,
Although against her will, as it appears
In the true course of all the question.

Antonio Well, I am glad that all things sort so well.

Benedick And so am I, being else by faith enforced
To call young Claudio to a reckoning for it.

Leonato Well daughter, and you gentlewomen all,
Withdraw into a chamber by yourselves,
And when I send for you, come hither masked.
The Prince and Claudio promised by this hour
To visit me. You know your office, brother,
You must be father to your brother's daughter,
And give her to young Claudio.

The women exit.

Antonio Which I will do with confirmed countenance.

Benedick Friar, I must entreat your pains, I think.

Friar To do what signor?

Benedick To bind me, or undo me, one of them.
Signor Leonato, truth it is, good signor,
Your niece regards me with an eye of favour.

Leonato That eye my daughter lent her, 'tis most true.

Benedick And I do with an eye of love requite her.

3 **Upon the error that you heard debated:** misled, as you have had explained
5 **against her will:** not on purpose
6 **all the question:** the investigation
7 **sort:** have turned out
8 **by faith:** because of my promise
9 **call young Claudio to a reckoning:** challenge Claudio to a duel
14 **office:** role
17 **confirmed countenance:** a straight face
18 **entreat your pains:** ask you to do something for me
20 **To bind me, or undo me:** puns on tying/untying, meaning marry him
22 **regards me with an eye of favour:** seems to like me
23 **That eye my daughter lent her:** thanks to Hero's intervention
24 **requite her:** return her love

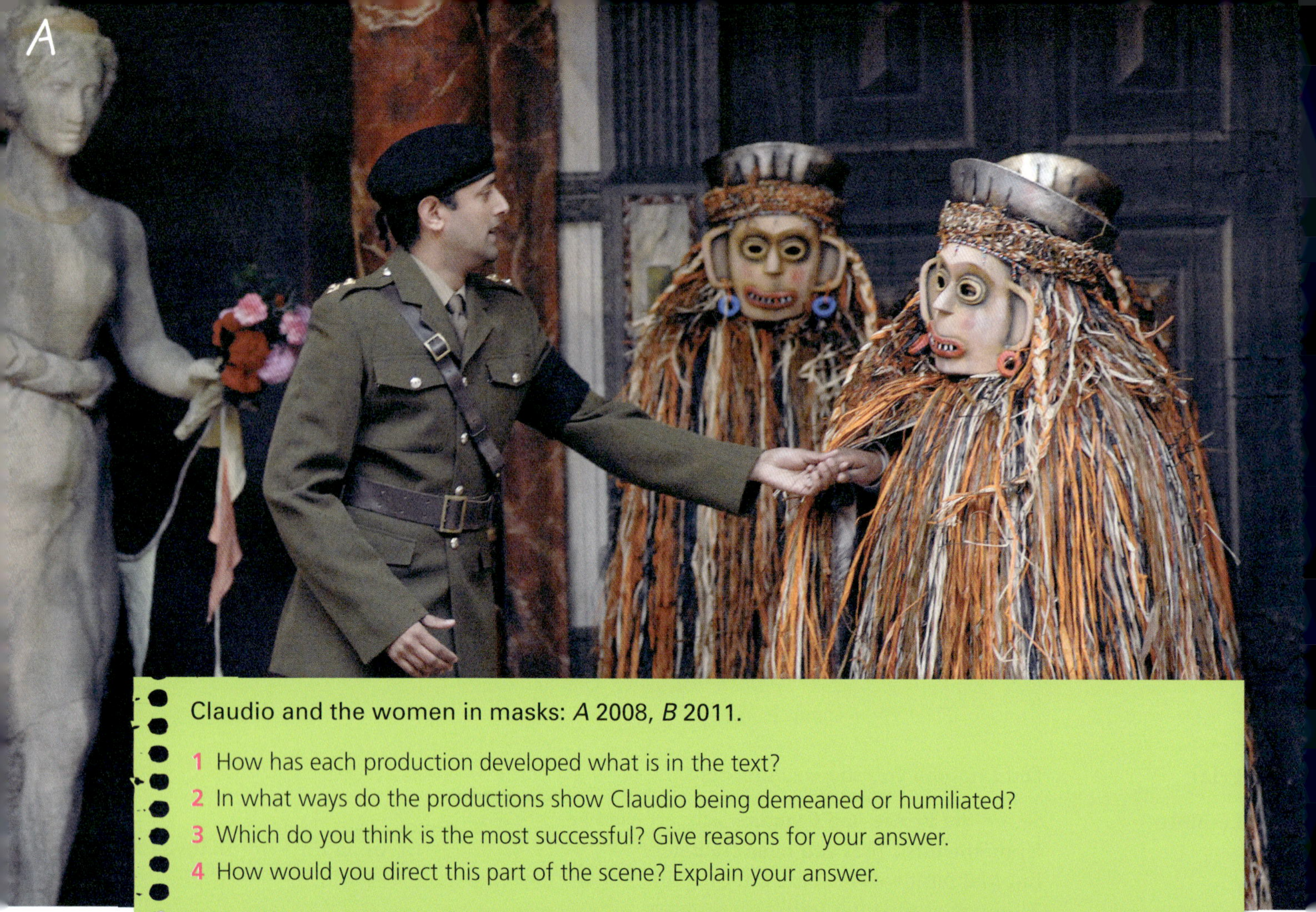

Claudio and the women in masks: *A* 2008, *B* 2011.

1 How has each production developed what is in the text?
2 In what ways do the productions show Claudio being demeaned or humiliated?
3 Which do you think is the most successful? Give reasons for your answer.
4 How would you direct this part of the scene? Explain your answer.

A Navin Chowdhry; ***B*** Philip Cumbus

Leonato
The sight whereof I think you had from me,
From Claudio, and the Prince. But what's your will?

Benedick
Your answer sir is enigmatical.
But for my will, my will is, your good will
May stand with ours this day to be conjoined
In the state of honourable marriage,
In which, good Friar, I shall desire your help.

Leonato
My heart is with your liking.

Friar
And my help.
Here comes the Prince and Claudio.

Enter Don Pedro and Claudio with attendants.

Don Pedro
Good morrow to this fair assembly.

Leonato
Good morrow Prince, good morrow Claudio.
We here attend you. Are you yet determined
Today to marry with my brother's daughter?

Claudio
I'll hold my mind, were she an Ethiope.

Leonato
Call her forth brother, here's the Friar ready.

[Exit Antonio.]

Don Pedro
Good morrow Benedick. Why, what's the matter
That you have such a February face,
So full of frost, of storm, and cloudiness?

Claudio
I think he thinks upon the savage bull.
Tush, fear not, man, we'll tip thy horns with gold,
And all Europa shall rejoice at thee,
As once Europa did at lusty Jove,
When he would play the noble beast in love.

Benedick
Bull Jove sir, had an amiable low,
And some such strange bull leaped your father's cow,
And got a calf in that same noble feat
Much like to you, for you have just his bleat.

Claudio
For this I owe you.
Enter Antonio, Hero, Beatrice, Margaret, and Ursula, the women wearing masks.
Here comes other reck'nings.
Which is the lady I must seize upon?

Antonio
[Leading Hero forward.]
This same is she, and I do give you her.

Claudio
Why then she's mine. Sweet, let me see your face.

Leonato
No, that you shall not till you take her hand
Before this Friar, and swear to marry her.

Claudio
Give me your hand before this holy Friar,
I am your husband if you like of me.

Hero
[Unmasking.] And when I lived I was your other wife,
And when you loved, you were my other husband.

25 **The sight whereof I think you had from me:** you know that thanks to
26 **what's your will?:** what do you want?
27 **enigmatical:** puzzling (he doesn't realise they know he was listening to them)
28 **for:** as for
32 **My heart is with your liking:** I approve the marriage
38 **I'll hold my mind:** my mind's made up to do it
41 **February face:** cold, unsmiling expression
43 **the savage bull:** the horns of a cuckold
44 **tip thy horns with gold:** make you look a fine sacrificial bull
45 **Europa:** here means Europe
46 **Europa:** here means Europa, who in Greek legend was kidnapped by the god Zeus (Jove to the Romans) as a bull
48 **amiable low:** pleasant voice; he then uses bull imagery to suggest Claudio is not his father's son
52 **For this I owe you:** I'll pay you back for that remark
52 **other reck'nings:** other bills to be paid
59 **like of me:** want to marry me

Beatrice and Benedick, 2008.

Pick a point in the scene that you think is most likely to be the exact moment the photograph was taken, and explain the reasons for your choice.

Kirsty Besterman, Bill Buckhurst

FROM THE REHEARSAL ROOM...

LOVE ON THE LINE

This is a repeat of the activity on pages 10, 34, 50, 58 and 86. Look back for the instructions and to remind yourself of your previous answers.

- In pairs, read lines 74 to 96. One person reads Benedick, and the other Beatrice.
- Now, read again. This time, before you say your own lines, **repeat** the most important word that the other character said. Continue to the end of the extract.

1 Note or highlight all the words or phrases that were repeated.

- Read the extract again. Allow the word you repeat to really drive the way you say your next line.

2 How does Benedick react to Beatrice's responses? What does this reveal about his feelings for her?

3 Where is Beatrice on the line? Quote from the text to support your answer.

4 Where is Benedick on the line? Quote from the text to support your answer.

- Stand in the places on the line, and compare your answers with other groups. Use your quotes to support your views.

5 Record your answers, and those that the majority of the class agree on.

6 Compare all your judgements for Love on the Line. What journey does their relationship follow?

Claudio Another Hero!

Hero Nothing certainer.
One Hero died defiled, but I do live,
And surely as I live, I am a maid.

Don Pedro The former Hero! Hero that is dead!

Leonato She died, my lord, but whiles her slander lived.

Friar All this amazement can I qualify,
When, after that the holy rites are ended,
I'll tell you largely of fair Hero's death.
Meantime let wonder seem familiar,
And to the chapel let us presently.

Benedick Soft and fair, Friar. — Which is Beatrice?

Beatrice *[Unmasking.]* I answer to that name. What is your will?

Benedick Do not you love me?

Beatrice Why no, no more than reason.

Benedick Why, then your uncle, and the Prince, and Claudio
Have been deceived, they swore you did.

Beatrice Do not you love me?

Benedick Troth no, no more than reason.

Beatrice Why, then my cousin Margaret, and Ursula
Are much deceived, for they did swear you did.

Benedick They swore that you were almost sick for me.

Beatrice They swore that you were well-nigh dead for me.

Benedick 'Tis no such matter. Then you do not love me?

Beatrice No, truly, but in friendly recompense.

Leonato Come cousin, I am sure you love the gentleman.

Claudio And I'll be sworn upon't that he loves her,
For here's a paper written in his hand,
A halting sonnet of his own pure brain,
Fashioned to Beatrice.

Hero And here's another,
Writ in my cousin's hand, stolen from her pocket,
Containing her affection unto Benedick.

Benedick A miracle! Here's our own hands against our hearts. Come, I will have thee, but by this light I take thee for pity.

Beatrice I would not deny you, but by this good day I yield upon great persuasion, and partly to save your life, for I was told you were in a consumption.

Benedick Peace, I will stop your mouth. *[Kisses her.]*

Don Pedro How dost thou, Benedick, the married man?

63 **defiled:** disgraced by slander
66 **but whiles:** only while
67 **qualify:** explain
68 **after that the holy rites are ended:** once you are married
69 **largely:** in full
70 **let wonder seem familiar:** just accept it
72 **Soft and fair:** wait a minute
80 **for me:** with love for me
81 **well-nigh:** nearly
82 **'Tis no such matter:** nothing of the sort
83 **friendly recompense:** as a friend
87 **halting:** limping (because the verse does not scan)
87 **his own pure brain:** his own composing
95 **in a consumption:** wasting away (from love)

Actor's view

Philip Cumbus
Claudio, 2011

I think Claudio has a brilliant journey through the play. It's always exciting as an actor to have a journey that really goes somewhere, that travels a great distance from the man we meet at the beginning to the man we leave at the end. And I think Claudio, by the end, has learnt to think a bit harder.

I think he's learnt that a man who is not at war can't behave like a man at war. I think he's learnt to think before he acts, in a way I think he's learnt to be human again. I've found the whole concept of the soldier's life really interesting and how that affects Claudio and affects a lot of the things he does through the course of the play. And actually by the end he's found a sense of peace somehow, a sense of clarity of who he really is. Unfortunately, in order to get there, he's had to go through the most incredible drama and incredible emotional upheaval. But, at the end of it, he has found a shred of self confidence, a shred of belief in himself, that means he can stand up and he can acknowledge his own faults.

I think that it is a big deal for someone like Claudio to acknowledge his own faults and to acknowledge that he has done something wrong. And the play finishes with that tone: it's celebratory, it's joyous, it's loving, but the whole thing for Claudio is tainted by a slight sense of all that he did wrong and I think it's quite nice that he is left with that.

Actor's view

Mariah Gale
Hero, 2004

Claudio says, when he realises the truth about what has happened, 'dispose for hence forth of poor Claudio.' That is when he accepts Leonato's wishes for him to marry her supposed cousin. A lot of people say that's awful that he says, 'all right then, I'll marry someone else,' but I think that what that is, a sacrifice. He's saying, 'well, she's gone and so I will marry someone else who I've never set eyes on before and it won't be about that love, it will just be punishment.' I think it's interesting that he says, 'right, ok, I'm accepting this' and that's the death of a young Claudio that he lays himself to rest and takes on a new life.

I think it's a rite of passage for both of them that they have never been heartbroken and isn't that one of the biggest lessons you learn, isn't that one of the things that makes you grow up so much? And I think that is what happens to them, they get shattered, but the nice thing is that it's a happy ending because they go through heartbreak and they are reunited. I mean, that's wonderful.

The cast in the final dance, 2011.

Benedick I'll tell thee what, Prince. A college of wit-crackers cannot flout me out of my humour. Dost thou think I care for a satire or an epigram? No, if a man will be beaten with brains, 'a shall wear nothing handsome about him. In brief, since I do purpose to marry, I will think nothing to any purpose that the world can say against it, and therefore never flout at me for what I have said against it. For man is a giddy thing, and this is my conclusion. For thy part Claudio, I did think to have beaten thee, but in that thou art like to be my kinsman, live unbruised, and love my cousin.

Claudio I had well hoped thou wouldst have denied Beatrice, that I might have cudgelled thee out of thy single life, to make thee a double-dealer, which out of question thou wilt be if my cousin do not look exceeding narrowly to thee.

Benedick Come, come, we are friends. Let's have a dance ere we are married, that we may lighten our own hearts and our wives' heels.

Leonato We'll have dancing afterward.

Benedick First, of my word, therefore play music. Prince, thou art sad. Get thee a wife, get thee a wife! There is no staff more reverent than one tipped with horn.

Enter Messenger.

Messenger My lord, your brother John is ta'en in flight,
And brought with armed men back to Messina.

Benedick Think not on him till tomorrow. I'll devise thee brave punishments for him. Strike up, pipers!

They dance.

99 **flout me out of my humour:** upset me by mocking

101 **'a:** he

102 **purpose:** intend

103 **to any purpose:** worth acting on

107 **in that:** because

107 **like to be my kinsman:** about to become a relative

108 **my cousin:** Hero

110 **cudgelled:** beaten

111 **a double-dealer:** an unfaithful husband

111 **out of question:** certainly

112 **my cousin:** Beatrice

112 **look exceeding narrowly to:** keep a close eye on

117 **of my word:** I insist

118–9 **There is no staff … tipped with horn:** You need a wife, even if you might become a cuckold

122 **brave:** fitting

SHAKESPEARE'S WORLD

Ending with a dance

We have an eyewitness account of a performance of a play at the original Globe. In 1599, the year it opened, Thomas Platter, a Swiss traveller, went to a performance one afternoon in September. He wrote about it in his diary:

> *After dinner, about 2 o'clock, I went with my companions over the water, and in the thatched playhouse saw the tragedy of Julius [Caesar] with at least 15 characters, very well acted. At the end of the performance, they danced according to their custom, with extreme elegance.*

In *Much Ado About Nothing* this dance fits into the story at the end of the play.

Director's Note, 5.4

- ✔ As people gather for the wedding, Benedick asks Leonato for his permission to marry Beatrice.
- ✔ The women enter masked, Claudio agrees to marry Antonio's niece without seeing her face.
- ✔ Hero tells him he is marrying her after all.
- ✔ Beatrice unmasks, but she and Benedick can't quite admit, publicly, that they love one another.
- ✔ Claudio and Hero prove they do, showing poems Beatrice and Benedick had written about each other.
- ✔ They dance, before going on to hold a double wedding.

STUDY NOTES, 5.4

TIP

A good response

A good response may make links between details in a scene and details in a scene before or after. This can show either that Shakespeare is sustaining an aspect of plot or character (i.e. doing something to reinforce it) or developing an aspect of plot character (i.e. making it more varied or complex).

For example, Shakespeare could have made Benedick simply a comic character who has changed his mind about Beatrice, love and marriage, but he uses him to show that a man may have to choose between his partner and his close friend. Shakespeare also uses Benedick as the voice of a final truth that may be part of the play's main message: 'for man is a giddy thing, and this is my conclusion'.

TIP

Writing about drama

- An example of Shakespeare providing cues for the emphasis of line delivery can be seen in lines 41–2: 'a **Feb**ruary **face**, so **full** of **frost**, of **storm**, and **cloud**iness'. Commenting on how lines have been written for delivery with rhythm and impact shows you understand this aspect of performance.
- Dramatic writing has to keep an audience engaged. Chart the different moods, characters and settings covered in any one of the five acts to see how Shakespeare keeps his audience engaged.

1 Character and plot development

The last scene of a play may show a major change in the way a character has been developed, or it may simply show how parts of the plot are resolved. In this case, Claudio is the character who is most developed, and the scene is concerned with tying up various parts of the plot; e.g. wrongs righted, lovers united, villains defeated and a happy ending.

1 Shakespeare begins the scene with the Friar's statement about Hero's innocence, and Leonato declaring the Prince and Claudio innocent because they had been deceived. Does this present Leonato the same as he has been, or as someone who has changed?
2 Benedick asks Leonato to approve his proposed marriage to Beatrice, Leonato's niece. How does Shakespeare make Benedick seem reluctant to declare his love passionately and personally in lines 22 and 24?
3 Claudio believes he has to marry Leonato's niece (who he has never met) as an act of blind commitment, whereas he hoped to marry Hero from love. Do you think Claudio's attitude shows him as ashamed, or trapped? (See line 53, and earlier in Act 5 Scene 1 lines 226–77.)
4 How does Shakespeare remind the audience of the previous relationship between Benedick and Beatrice (lines 74–83)?
5 When their private writings about each other are brought out to prove their love, they continue their pretence of not liking each other. How does Shakespeare create this in lines 91–5?

2 Characterisation and voice: dramatic language

Shakespeare usually provides some clear cues to how lines may be delivered by putting in a pattern of exclamations, pauses, or emphatic words that help an actor to find the appropriate voice for lines. However, some lines are open to a range of possible vocalisation, and it is for the actor and director to find the most effective way of voicing them.

6 When Hero takes off her mask and announces that 'I was your other wife' (line 60), Claudio says 'Another Hero!' (line 62). How could this be spoken to show different ways the actor might choose to react?
7 What kind of voices best suit the exchange between Claudio and Benedick in lines 43–52?

3 Themes and ideas

The two plots of the play (Benedick and Beatrice and Hero and Claudio) have some common themes, such as true love tested, obstructed but triumphant, and the way that 'much ado' can arise out of various kinds of 'nothing'. What makes the play a comedy rather than a tragedy is that it shows that, whatever the obstacles or 'much ado', things can and do work out for the best in the end. Reconciliation is not only a way of bringing the events of the play to a neat conclusion, but is also a major theme in the play.

8 Do you think that Shakespeare's ending to the play is intended to show that forgiveness is the reward for remorse?

STUDY NOTES, 5.4

9 How many kinds of reconciliation do you find in the final scene?

10 What aspects of love do you think Shakespeare presents in this scene?

4 Performance

Actors and directors can choose what parts of a play's themes or actions to emphasise, and how to put an interpretation on lines that may not be immediately clear. They also have to decide what keeps an audience interested, through humour or suspense. More basically, they need to make actors interesting to watch even when they are not speaking their lines.

11 Beatrice and Hero have no lines in the opening part of the scene. How might their performance show how they respond to what they hear, and how might they exit the stage after line 16 to prepare for what follows, and enter again at line 52?

12 How would you advise an acting company to play the unveiling scene?

13 What advice would you give to the actors playing Benedick and Beatrice when Hero and Claudio bring out their private letters in lines 85–90?

14 How might Benedick and Claudio play their lines 109–15, when they are reunited in friendship?

5 Contexts and responses

The way audiences respond to a play can vary according to choices made by actors and directors. They may also vary according to the general attitudes, opinions and beliefs held by a particular group, or common to all groups at the time of watching the play.

15 What meanings and messages do you think different members of the audience may find in Shakespeare's final scene of the play?

6 Reflecting on the play

16 'Shakespeare's presentation of Beatrice in the final scene is disappointingly weaker than it was before.' Do you think that Beatrice is presented differently in this scene, and that the difference is disappointing?

17 '*Much Ado About Nothing* was, in its time, a successful comic entertainment but it has little to show any insight into human relationships today.' How far is this a fair or unfair comment about the play?

18 How has your understanding and appreciation of the play been affected by seeing it performed on stage or screen?

USING THE VIDEO

Exploring interpretation and performance

If you have looked at the video extracts in the online version try these questions.

- In the 2011 production Claudio is blindfolded, and there is comical stage business between Claudio and the women. When Hero reveals herself, the audience laughs. Do you think this approach:
  - a) spoils the serious aspect of the scene?
  - b) is along the lines of what Shakespeare intended?
- The audience obviously enjoyed the scene where Benedick and Beatrice are at last united. List five things in the performance that provide humour from what we see on stage, not just from what we hear.

TIP

Reflecting on the play

When writing about a character in a play, remember to comment on how he or she may show motives, feelings and reactions that are typical of ordinary people, or even ourselves. This helps to show appreciation of Shakespeare's skill in showing common human elements in characters on stage – and making us sometimes empathise with them as well as judge them.

1.1	A messenger tells Leonato that Don Pedro (the Prince) has returned victorious from the war (with Claudio, who has become a war hero, and Benedick). When they arrive, Leonato asks them to stay a month, including Don John (the Prince's Bastard brother) who was on the other side in the war, but is now reconciled. Benedick and Beatrice have their first 'duel of wit', both saying they dislike the opposite sex. Claudio tells Benedick he is in love with Hero (Leonato's daughter). The Prince tells Claudio she will inherit Leonato's fortune, and offers to woo her for Claudio.
1.2	Antonio tells Leonato his servant has heard the Prince plan to woo Hero (for himself).
1.3	Borachio tells Don John he has (correctly) overheard the plan for the Prince to woo Hero for Claudio. Don John hates Claudio who was a key person in his defeat. He wants to wreck the marriage.
2.1	Beatrice says she will not marry, and Leonato encourages Hero to say yes if Don Pedro proposes. The men arrive masked, and Shakespeare gives us mini-scenes as the couples dance. In one Benedick mocks Beatrice, and she, pretending not to know it is Benedick, calls him the Prince's Fool. Don John tells Claudio the Prince has wooed Hero for himself. Claudio sulks, and is eventually told the truth by the Prince. Leonato insists Hero and Claudio must wait a week before their marriage, and the Prince plans to use this time by tricking Beatrice and Benedick into falling in love. Leonato, Claudio and Hero agree to help him.
2.2	Borachio comes up with a plan, which Don John welcomes, to fool Claudio into thinking Hero has a lover.
2.3	The first gulling scene. Benedick regrets the changes in Claudio since his love for Hero. He then hides, and the Prince, Leonato and Claudio talk about Beatrice's love for him, knowing he is listening to them. Benedick believes them, and decides to return Beatrice's love.
3.1	The second gulling scene. Hero and Ursula trick Beatrice into hearing them talk about Benedick's love for Beatrice, and her pride. When they leave Beatrice decides to change, and to love Benedick.
3.2	The Prince and Claudio tease Benedick because he has changed. Don John tells the Prince and Claudio that Hero has a lover, and he can show them when she lets a man in at her bedroom window that night.
3.3	In a comic scene, the foolish Dogberry and Verges instruct the Watch in their duties. Borachio boasts to Conrade about how well the plan to ruin Hero has worked, and how much money Don John has given him. The Watch overhear them, and despite not quite understanding all that has been said, arrest them.
3.4	Margaret dresses Hero for the wedding. Beatrice says she has a cold, but they tease her for being in love.
3.5	Dogberry and Verges tell Leonato about the arrest of Borachio and Conrade, but they make so little sense that he tells them to question the prisoners themselves, because he is rushing to get to Hero's wedding.
4.1	The wedding. Claudio refuses to marry Hero, claiming she is not a virgin. The Prince backs up his story, and they leave. Leonato blames Hero, who faints, but the Friar believes she is innocent and has a plan – to pretend Hero is dead and find out the truth. Leonato agrees, and they go to hide Hero in a convent. Left on stage Benedick and Beatrice admit they love each other, and she persuades him to challenge Claudio to a duel.
4.2	Dogberry makes a mess of questioning Borachio and Conrade, but the Sexton takes over and finds out what really happened. He goes off to tell Leonato.
5.1	Leonato and Antonio, both very upset, try to challenge Claudio to a duel, but he refuses to take them seriously. They leave, and Benedick appears, and does challenge Claudio to a duel. Dogberry arrives with his prisoners and the Prince and Claudio find out what really happens. Leonato returns, and they both beg his forgiveness. Claudio agrees to marry Leonato's seeming 'niece'.
5.2	Benedick writes a poem to Beatrice. She arrives. Ursula brings the news of the discovery of the plot.
5.3	Claudio mourns Hero at what he thinks is her tomb.
5.4	Claudio finds out his bride is really Hero. Benedick and Beatrice agree to marry, but only after Claudio and Hero stop them arguing by producing the poems they have written. They all dance before the weddings.

Key terms

These key terms provide a starting place for exploring key aspects of *Much Ado About Nothing*. Your teacher will tell you which examples are most relevant to how your Shakespeare response will be assessed.

THEMES AND IDEAS

Concealment

Don Pedro conceals his identity to woo Hero on Claudio's behalf 1.1. 261–4; 2.1. 72

Benedick 2.3 and Beatrice 3.1 are concealed when tricked to think each love the other;

Hero is concealed after Claudio accuses her of being unfaithful 4.1. 103 until her honour is restored 5.4 and Claudio's punishment for dishonouring her is complete

Hero and Beatrice are concealed for Hero's marriage to Claudio in his belief that she is Hero's cousin 5.4 52–9

Beatrice and Benedick conceal their feelings for each other when the gulling is revealed, but their love notes show their true love and lead to marriage 5.4. 72–115

Conflict

Aggression/violence

Male soldiers fight and kill 1.1. 5–40; Claudio is aggressive as he thinks he's lost Hero 2.1. 166–174

Believing his daughter is disgraced, Leonato threatens violence against: himself 4.1. 106, 'impure' Hero 4.1. 19–26, 190–1; then against her false accusers 4.1. 191–201; 5.1. 53–71

Violence is needed to avenge Hero's honour so Leonato 5.1. 66, then Antonio 5.1.80–6, and finally Benedick 5.1. 140–4 challenge Claudio to a duel 5.1. 140–82

Hatred/jealousy

Conflict has serious consequences for Claudio, Hero and Leonato when hatred and jealousy drive Don John, the Bastard brother of Don Pedro, to enmity 1.3. 22–33; Don John is jealous of Claudio's favoured position 1.3. 52–5 and wants revenge, resulting in a sequence of events where Claudio believes Don Pedro courts Hero for himself and is jealous 2.1. 147–57 but does nothing about it; then Don John deceives Claudio to believe that Hero is unfaithful 2.2. 26–45, 3.2. 66–114; 3.3. 130–47 and his jealousy causes him to disgrace her publicly 4.1. 80–105 resulting in the breakdown in friendship between Claudio and Benedick who promises Beatrice to 'kill Claudio'; and in Hero's supposed death 4.1. 285–328

Merry war

Conflict between Beatrice and Benedick entertains with a witty, humorous 'merry war' of words 1.1. 49–51; 96–120; 2.1. 109–29, although Beatrice's words hurt 2.1. 214–5

Conflict within Beatrice and Benedick about love and marriage is shown when they say they will never love or marry 1.1. 102–9, 197–224; 2.1. 23–56; 2.1. 207–27; 2.3. 8–35; contrasted with their love of each other revealed in the gulling scenes and the love they declare to each other 2.3. 36–238, 3.1. 1–117; 4.1. 225–84; leading Beatrice to persuade Benedick to 'kill Claudio' 4.1. 285–328

Once they agree to marry, they find out they were tricked into declaring their love, resulting in exchanges 5.4. 72–95 that echo the wit earlier in the play, which Benedick stops with a kiss 5.4. 96

Deception

Comic

Claudio, Don Pedro and Leonato gull Benedick into believing Beatrice loves him 2.3. 36–238; Hero and Ursula gull Beatrice into believing Benedick loves her 3.1. 1–117; leading them to confess their love for each other 4.1. 266–84 and to marriage 5.4. 96–119

Serious

Don John deceives Don Pedro and his followers into believing they are reconciled 1.1. 129; 1.3. 15–21 but hatred 1.3. 22–31 drives him to fight on 1.3. 52–5 and attempt to flee when his plans fail 5.4. 120–1

Don John deceives Claudio that Don Pedro woos Hero for himself 2.1. 133–46 and that Hero is unfaithful 3.2. 73–114; Borachio courts Margaret who is dressed in Hero's clothes, to deceive 2.2. 26–48; 3.2. 66–114; 3.3. 130–147; which is later revealed 5.1. 213–25

The deception destroys Claudio's love 3.3. 143–47; Hero's honour and marriage 4.1; brings dishonour to Don Pedro 4.1. 59–61; and to Leonato's family and status 4.1. 119–42

Leonato deceives Claudio that Hero died of shame 5.1 58–71, and Claudio must make amends by clearing her name 5.1. 261–67 and marrying her seeming 'cousin' 5.1. 268–77

Self deception

Benedick claims in his first soliloquy in 2.3 that he will never love or marry; in his next soliloquy, after the gulling, he decides that he will now love and marry but deceives himself it is only because the world 'must be peopled' 2.3. 199–222; he then deceives himself into believing that Beatrice's antagonism when calling him for dinner reveals her love for him 2.3. 223–38

Beatrice deceives herself that she will never submit to a husband 2.1. 49–56 but after the gulling declares her love, writes love notes, then when the gulling comes to light deceives by saying she only loves him in 'friendly recompense' 5.4. 83 until the love notes come to light and Benedick stops her mouth with a kiss 5.4. 96

Gender

Men

Fight 1.1. 5–14, pursue women 1.1. 32–5, hold power over women as fathers 2.1. 57–8, and husbands 2.1. 51–4; decide who should marry 1.1. 259–64, 2.1. 57–8, 5.1. 268–73

It is a man's duty to avenge insult on women: e.g. Leonato 5.1. 58–71, then Antonio 5.1. 80–3 and finally Benedick 5.1. 140–82 challenge Claudio to duel over Hero's honour

Benedick seems different from other men – suspicious of marriage 1.1. 197–204; mocks Claudio for falling in love 2.3. 8–35; is then tricked into love with Beatrice and explains his change of heart in a practical way, 'the world must be peopled' 2.3. 36–222; is then prepared to 'kill Claudio' at Beatrice's request 4.1. 285–328; is ready to marry Beatrice, stopping her witty words with a kiss 5.4. 96

In contrast to Benedick, Claudio seems an idealistic man in love who reveres Hero and desires marriage 1.1. 149, 155, 249–68; with high principles which are dashed by the deceit of Don John, leading to accusation that Hero is unfaithful 4.1 and subsequent penitence when he believes Hero is dead, agreeing to restore her honour and marry a woman he's told is Hero's cousin 5.1. 261–77; leading to reconciliation with Benedick, Hero's family and Hero herself as she reveals her identity 5.4

Women

Stay at home while soldiers fight, wait to be wooed and hope for marriage 1.1; should submit to fathers and husbands 2.1. 43–58, respond silently to male oppression 4.1

Beatrice seems different from other women, with intellect and wit equal to a man's: e.g. mocking Benedick in a 'merry war' 1.1. 25–74

Beatrice initially rejects love 1.1. 107–9 and is reluctant to marry 2.1. 51–6; women's status means she cannot avenge the attack on Hero's honour but her words persuade Benedick to 'kill Claudio' 4.1. 286–328

In contrast to Beatrice, Hero does not join in witty exchanges in 1.1, speaking only in line 30; seems quiet and submissive, compliant when Don Pedro courts her in Claudio's name 2.1. 72–82, 259–72; of few words when Claudio accuses her of being unfaithful in 4.1 and forgiving after Claudio proclaims her innocence, agreeing to marry him 5.4. 60–4

Love

Marriage

Necessary for lovers and society's well being 2.3. 199–220 and honoured 3.4. 26–34

Initially marriage is perceived as a trap by Benedick 1.1. 163–8 and Beatrice 2.1. 51–69

Marriages are arranged by men: e.g. Claudio chooses Hero 1.1. 243, Don Pedro gains Hero for Claudio 1.1. 259–64, 2.1. 72–82, 258–65

Leonato arranges for penitent Claudio to marry his seeming 'niece' 5.1. 261–73

True love

Achieved when people really know one another: e.g. when Claudio knows Hero's honesty 5.1. 213–27, 233–4, and is penitent 5.1. 253–7; when Beatrice and Benedick know each other's love 4.1. 266–85, 5.4. 73–96, overcoming their former fears of constraint 1.1. 199–204, 2.1. 51–6

Trust/mistrust

Beatrice hints that she loved Benedick but he let her down: 1.1. 120; 2.1. 243–49; the threat of mistrust destroying Beatrice and Benedick's love is overcome by the truth in their notes 5.4. 73–96

Claudio's mistrust 4.1. 52–8 ruins Hero but she is saved by the Friar's trust 4.1. 154–69 and defended by the trust of Beatrice and Benedick 4.1. 255–328

Nothing/Noting

The title, theme and pun of nothing/ noting/'no-thing' runs through the play: 'Much Ado' is made about 'Nothing' as nothing is as it seems – Don Pedro's reported wooing of Hero 2.1. 139–57; Hero seemingly talking to a lover 3.3. 130–47, 5.1. 102–5, 213–28; the reported love of Beatrice and Benedick 2.3. 88–189, 3.1. 1–117; Hero's 'death' 4.1. 201–8; Claudio's wedding 5.4. 53–65

'No-thing' (a slang reference to the vagina at the time) links with the deception that Hero is unfaithful whereas she is innocent 5.1. 213–28

Noting: Claudio 'notes' Hero 1.1. 133–5 and Don John then schemes so Hero is wrongly noticed with another man 3.3. 130–47

The lead up to Balthasar's song plays on noting, nothing and notes, leading to the song that 'men are deceivers ever' 2.3. 36–76

Remorse/Reconciliation/ Forgiveness

The truth of Hero's innocence reconciles Leonato to her 5.1. 41–71

Claudio shows remorse, seeks forgiveness 5.1. 228, 261–77, 5.4. 53–65 and is rewarded with Hero

Beatrice and Benedick are reconciled through the truth of their love for each other 5.4. 85–96

Don Pedro's reconciliation and forgiveness towards Don John 1.1. 128–9 is spurned, he shows no remorse for his behaviour 1.3. 8–31, and is recaptured after fleeing 5.4. 120

Reputation/Honour/Dishonour

Man's honour is established in fighting 1.1. 5–14

Don John's dishonoured position as the bastard brother of Prince Don Pedro leads to his bitterness 1.3, deception of Claudio and dishonouring of Hero 2.1. 133–57, 3.3. 130–47

Women's honour, reputation and position in society depends on sexual purity so Hero's supposed unfaithfulness dishonours Claudio 4.1 and Leonato who cares more for the loss of family honour than Hero's suffering 4.1. 119–42; and is symbolised in Hero's supposed death 5.1. 62–71

Honour is stirred up against Claudio to avenge Hero's dishonour in a duel: Leonato 5.1. 58–71; Antonio 80–5; and Benedick 140–85 challenge Claudio

Hero's reputation is restored when the truth of deceit is revealed 5.1. 213–27, reparation is agreed 5.1. 261–72 and Hero is cleared of dishonour 5.3

Claudio keeps his promise to marry Hero's supposed cousin resulting in an honourable end when Hero reveals her identity 5.4. 60 and Don John is captured in flight 5.4. 120

CHARACTERISATION/VOICE

Characterisation

The skill of making an actor playing a part do it so well that the audience believes he is a real person, with a distinct personality, attitudes, feelings and behaviour. Characterisation can be developed by reported details: e.g. of Beatrice 2.1. 298–307 or by revealed behaviour: e.g. Don John, 1.3. 8–31

Voice *see Examiner's Tip p 20*

LANGUAGE

Blank verse

Verse with a regular pattern of emphasis which is not written in rhyme but helps the actor speak the lines: 'You **seem** to **me** as **Di**ane **in** her **orb**,/As **chaste** as **is** the **bud** ere **it** be **blown**' 4.1. 53–4

Imagery

Language chosen to put vivid, usually visual images in the audience's head: e.g.

Alliteration

Repetition of the same consonant sounds, especially at the beginning of words: e.g. Benedick with a '**F**ebruary **f**ace, so **f**ull of **f**rost' 5.4. 41–2

Animal imagery
Used in the 'war of words': e.g. Benedick calls Beatrice a parrot-teacher 1.1. 115; Beatrice describes Benedick as ending with a 'jade's trick' 1.1. 120 Benedick's links with love and marriage are linked with a bull from 1.1. 219 and carried through the play to 5.4. 43–51
When gulling Benedick, Claudio says 'this fish will bite' 2.3. 104; when gulling Beatrice, Ursula refers to 'pleasant angling' of the fish 3.1. 26; Beatrice speaks of Benedick 'taming my wild heart' 3.1. 113
Used to insult: e.g. Don John calls Hero a 'forward march chick' 1.3. 45; Claudio compares Hero to a 'pamp'red animal' 4.1. 57–8
Used to praise: e.g. Claudio does 'in the figure of a lamb, the feats of a lion'; 1.1. 12–3
Used to describe evil: e.g. Don John as a caged animal 1.3. 27–8
Food/appetite imagery
E.g. Benedick compares Claudio's words of love to a 'fantastical banquet'; he claims love will not make an 'oyster' out of him 2.3. 20–5
Jealous Claudio is 'civil as an orange' 2.1. 256; discredited Hero a 'rotten orange' 4.1. 29
Don John's scheme is 'poison' 2.2. 18 so that Hero seems a 'contaminated stale' 2.2. 22; the speech revealing Hero's innocence causes Claudio to drink 'poison' while he uttered it 5.1. 228
Margaret notes to Beatrice that despite his heart Benedick will 'eat his meat' 3.4. 75
Extended metaphor
E.g. Beatrice's witty image of marriage as a Scotch jig 2.1. 62–8 Leonato of Hero's dishonour: 'fall'n into a pit of ink' that the wide sea cannot clean again 1.1 38–140

Irony
Used for humour: Benedick's soliloquy 2.3. 8–35 that he will never love or marry; contrasted by his next soliloquy 2.3. 199–222 that he will; used to increase tension: e.g. the audience see that Leonato might discover the plot to discredit Hero 3.5 but he misses the chance 4.1

Prose
The language of everyday speech, without a crafted formal pattern. Often used by characters of a lower social status , e.g. the Watch 3.3

Puns/word play/malapropisms
Add humour, entertainment and ambiguous meanings: e.g. witty puns such as Benedick as 'a stuffed man' 1.1. 47; Claudio as a 'civil orange' 2.1. 256; word play: e.g. on the meanings of 'notes' 2.3. 52–6; malapropisms: e.g. Dogberry says the villain will be 'condemned into everlasting redemption' (meaning the opposite, damnation) 4.2. 49–50; he requests that the villain will 'suspect' Dogberry (meaning the opposite, respect)

Verse
In this play verse is often used more formally: e.g. by Don Pedro 1.1. 259–81 or to describe love: e.g. Claudio 1.1. 250–69; Beatrice 3.1. 108–17; or to reveal high emotion: e.g. Claudio's soliloquy 2.1. 147–57

PERFORMANCE: STAGECRAFT AND THEATRICALITY

Stage directions
Shakespeare writes very few stage directions for an individual actor. Stage directions such as: 1.1 '*Don Pedro and Leaonato speak privately*' allow the audience to focus on Beatrice and Benedick's exchanges. However, Shakespeare does embed directions in his text as cues to actors: e.g. Leonato's instructions to Hero, Beatrice and the women to 'withdraw into the chamber' and 'when I send for you come hither masked' 5.4. 10–2

Structure
The way a play is built with different parts doing different jobs, such as setting the scene, and introducing or developing a character or plot: e.g. in this play plot parallels are used to create dramatic structure: Beatrice and Benedick's relationship mirrors Claudio and Hero's as they love, encounter obstacles, and find true love; the gulling of Benedick 2.3 is followed by the gulling of Beatrice 3.1

CONTEXTS

Contexts within the play (scene/mood)
E.g. in 2.3 and 3.1 the humorous gulling scenes are in the garden, where Beatrice and Benedick are hidden; in 4.1 solemnity for marriage at the church with Claudio's denouncement of Hero 4.1

Context around the play
The way that ideas, customs and events of the Elizabethan period, around 1598–9 are reflected in the play. *See* Shakespeare's World boxes.

Playing Shakespeare with Deutsche Bank

The 2008 production of *Much Ado About Nothing*, which features in this book, was the 2008 Playing Shakespeare with Deutsche Bank production. This is Globe Education's flagship programme for London schools, with 16,000 free tickets given to students for a full-scale Shakespeare production created specifically for young people.

www.playingshakespeare.org

Globe Education Shakespeare

Series Editors: Fiona Banks, Paul Shuter, Patrick Spottiswoode

Steering Committee: Fiona Banks, Hayley Bartley, Paul Shuter, Patrick Spottiswoode, Shirley Wakley

Much Ado About Nothing

Editors: Fiona Banks, Paul Shuter

Consultant: Shirley Wakley

Play text: Hayley Bartley, Paul Shuter, Patrick Spottiswoode

Glossary: Jane Shuter

Assessment: Peter Thomas, Paula Adair, Tony Farrell; key terms index: Clare Constant

From the rehearsal room: Fiona Banks, Adam Coleman, Sarah Nunn, Yolanda Vazquez

Shakespeare's World Farah Karim-Cooper, Sarah Dustagheer, Gwilym Jones, Amy Kenny, Paul Shuter

Dynamic Learning: Hayley Bartley

Progression: Georghia Ellinas, Michael Jones

Globe Education would like to thank our dedicated team of Globe Education Practitioners – who daily bring rehearsal room practices into the classroom for young people at Shakespeare's Globe and around the world. Their work is the inspiration for this series.

Photo credits
All photographs are from the Shakespeare's Globe Photo library.

John Tramper, 2004 production: 12, 32, 48, 56, 58, 62, 77, 88, 108; Andy Bradshaw, 2008 production: 10, 28, 30, 40, 48, 52, 58, 62, 82, 92, 102, 108, 110, 114, 116, 118; Manuel Harlan 2011 production: 5, 8, 10, 14, 16, 18,10, 28, 30, 34, 36, 38, 42, 46, 50, 52, 58, 64, 67, 74, 76, 80, 84, 86, 92, 94, 97, 100, 104, 106, 108, 110, 112, 116, 121; Pete le May: 4

Orders: please contact shakespeare@s-e-t.de

First published in Germany in 2012 by
S-E-T Studienreisen
Birkenstraße 37
28195 Bremen

Impression number 5 4 3 2 1
Year 2017 2016 2015 2014 2013 2012

Cover photo © Andy Bradshaw
Illustrations by DC Graphic Design Limited, Swanley Village, Kent
Garth Graphic Regular 10pt by DC Graphic Design Limited, Swanley Village, Kent
Printed in the UK by Bell & Bain Ltd.

ISBN: 978 3981 490909